Our Federation

Brisbane: Patriotism, Passion and Protest

1901

Edited by Barry Shaw

Brisbane History Group
Papers No. 18 ~ 2001

First published by:

National Library of Australia Cataloguing-in-Publication Data:

Our Federation 1901 : Brisbane : patriotism, passion and protest

Includes index
ISBN 0 9586255 3 0

ISSN 1031 7961

I. Brisbane (Qld) - History - 1891-1901. I. Shaw, Barry, 1947-. II. Brisbane History Group. (Series : Papers (Brisbane History Group) ; no. 18)

994.31032

Edited by Barry Shaw
Designed and typeset by Renee Strong & Ian Dillon
Printed by University of Queensland Printery
Produced by UQ Applied History Centre
Assisted by a Federation Community Projects Program Grant

1901-2001
A Federation Fund Project
A Commonwealth Government Initiative

Published by Brisbane History Group (Incorporated)
PO Box 12, Kelvin Grove DC
Qld 4059 Australia

Contents

Contributors

David Cameron, whose doctoral thesis examined the economy in Queensland, is a project officer with the Queensland Government.

Raymond Evans, reader in history at UQ, has written extensively on conflict and race in Queensland.

John Laverty, emeritus professor and past president of BHG, has written on local government in Brisbane.

John Mackenzie-Smith, possessing a doctorate from UQ, has researched and written on colonial Brisbane and the Scottish influence.

Katherine McConnel is researching for her PhD at UQ working on the history of federation in Queensland.

Bill Oliver, formerly an engineer, is an active member of the Brisbane History Group management committee and the Institution of Engineers, Australia.

Joanne Scott, lecturer in Australian Studies at the University of the Sunshine Coast, is co-authoring a history of the Queensland Premier's Department.

Barry Shaw, Honorary Research Adviser at UQ, is publications editor for the Brisbane History Group.

Illustrations

Preface

During 2001 the Brisbane History Group held a number of events to coincide with Australia's centenary of federation celebrations. In February our AGM was primarily an appetiser and looked at images of Brisbane on film and photograph at the turn of the century. In June we held a federation tour of Brisbane which included many hitherto neglected and yet significant sites and places. Nicely positioned between these two events was our more formal day, 'Brisbane and Federation'.

Held on 21 April 2001 at the Legislative Council Chamber, Parliament House, Brisbane, the focus was again on Queensland's capital, but the range of papers was broad, from politicians to poets and from commerce to conflict. This volume includes the papers delivered on that day. They have been supplemented by Joanne Scott's paper, 'Federation: The view from the Chief Secretary's Department', which provides an insight into what was happening in the upper echelons of Queensland government at the time.

A theme which appears and re-appears throughout this volume is the notion of continuity and change. True, federation did bring about change but much of it was ephemeral. Often the change occurred as the result of a combination of factors, and not just as a result of federation. The downturn in Brisbane manufacturing and primary industries was more to do with the prolonged and severe drought which afflicted Queensland from 1898 to 1903 rather than the ramifications of federation. Certainly federation had some impact, but many of the problems were long-standing. Inefficient plants reliant on outmoded machinery, a lack of financial development and government assistance were compounded by the drought-induced depression. Indeed recovery commenced after the drought had run its course.

The drought also affected certain Brisbane engineers at the turn of the century. Amid calls to reduce public servants' salaries because of the depressed state of the economy, engineers were required to focus on a multiplicity of tasks from dredging to drainage and from electrical supply to eradication of water hyacinth. On occasion they fell foul of their superiors. Henry Stanley's incorrectly aligned road bridge, a story which has parallels in 2001, possibly culminated in his removal, and Water Board engineer Alexander Stewart was apparently summarily dismissed when it was discovered he was suffering a life-threatening illness, no doubt induced by the conditions in which he worked. His replacement fared little better. After the expiration of his contract, Hugh Foster Barham was offered re-employment at a greatly reduced salary. Wholesale dismissals also occurred among Brisbane Municipal Council's engineers in 1900 after 'exhaustive enquiries'. The trials and tribulations of Brisbane engineers continue.

Changes in local government were mooted in the early 1890s well before federation. The Royal Commission on Local Government in 1896 made recommendations concerning the reduction of government endowments, the consolidation of local authorities, particularly in the Brisbane region, and the extension of their rating powers. These were changes already set in train by state and local governments, not by any impetus from federation.

At the state political level, change was certainly apparent in the Chief Secretary's Department immediately following federation. Certain roles and responsibilities, of necessity, altered and staff numbers fell dramatically. Yet many functions were retained, and even with regard to external affairs, Queensland still maintained its interests in immigration and its Agent-General's office in London which continued to be inordinately active.

A further, often underlying, theme in this volume is patriotism and protest. Both sides in the federation debate, the pro-federationists and anti-federationists, adopted a patriotic stance. This manifested itself in rousing national patriotic slogans such as 'One people, one destiny' and equally stirring parochial, and no less patriotic, catchcry of 'Queensland for the Queenslanders'. Moreover, as the crucial 2 September referendum loomed ever closer both sides grew increasingly passionate. War imagery began to appear in the newspapers, and terms like conflict and battle were used to describe the forthcoming vote.

Indeed the threat of impending federation produced a strange effect on some of the citizens of the capital. Normally tranquil Brisbane, 'a place where nothing ever happens', suddenly belied its carefree demeanour on the very eve of the referendum. There had been some hint of agitation at Centennial Hall in August 1899 when an angry audience had thrown a flag-waving federalist off the stage. But on 1 September agitation spawned outright aggression. At Centennial Hall Edmund Barton, Australia's future prime minister, was not only jostled by an angry crowd but later chased down the street. Another individual, mistaken for Barton, was unceremoniously pelted with eggs. Material damage included an overturned lorry and a room full of wrecked furniture.

Was this outburst of passion invoked by federation or merely an on going undercurrent of the violent protest which punctuates Brisbane from time to time? During the 1890s and 1900s there were certainly other episodes of protest, sectarian and xenophobic in character and quite unconnected with federation.

Federation also seemed to engender considerable animosity within the literary fraternity. The leading patriotic poets, George Essex Evans and James Brunton Stephens, were reviled by A.G. Stephens, the literary critic at the *Bulletin*, for their pompous and un-Australian versification. The situation deteriorated further when there were mutterings of prior arrangement and collusion concerning Essex Evans' award-winning 'Commonwealth ode', penned to celebrate federation. Yet, although the catalyst for the disputes might appear to be federation, it also had to do with the challenge to the traditional, inflated and imperial, some might argue imperious, poetry by the home-grown bush balladists.

Huge crowds assembled on 2 September 1899 as the referendum results were being posted on the large scoreboards erected outside the rival pro-federation Brisbane Courier and anti-federation Telegraph offices in Queen Street. While the state as a whole voted in favour of federation, the Brisbane electorates voted unanimously against. Of course, on New Years Day 1901 the streets were again packed as Brisbanites proudly celebrated federation. Patriotism, parochial and national, had achieved unity ... perhaps.

The Brisbane History Group is, as always, grateful to the authors who submitted their papers for this publication. All the papers were read by Rod Fisher, and Shirley McCorkindale proof read the entire volume.

A number of institutions have assisted with illustrations and information: Brisbane City Council, John Oxley Library, the Applied History Centre at the University of Queensland and the Institution of Engineers (Queensland).

This publication was made possible by a grant through the Commonwealth Goverment's Federation Community Projects Program. The BHG also thanks Arch Bevis, MHR for the Brisbane Electorate, and Ian Brusasco, chair of the select committee, for their support.

How to Vote for Federation.

THE BALLOT PAPER TO BE USED IN THE REFERENDUM ON SATURDAY IS SLIGHTLY DIFFERENT IN FORM FROM THAT EMPLOYED IN THE PARLIAMENTARY ELECTIONS, WHICH IS FAMILIAR TO EVERY VOTER. WE GIVE BELOW A REPRESENTATION OF THE REFERENDUM BALLOT PAPER AS IT WOULD APPEAR WHEN MARKED BY A VOTER IN FAVOUR OF FEDERATION. ALL THAT IS NECESSARY IN RECORDING A VOTE FOR THE COMMONWEALTH BILL IS TO DRAW THE PENCIL THROUGH THE WORD "NO" AS SHOWN:—

BALLOT PAPER.

ARE YOU IN FAVOUR OF THE PROPOSED FEDERAL CONSTITUTION BILL?

YES

~~NO~~

(If you are in favour of the Bill strike out the above word NO, as marked)

(If you are against the Bill strike out the above word YES).

0.1 How to vote for federation advertisement, *Brisbane courier* 1 Sep. 1899, 7

Politics & People

01 Brisbane
The key to federation?

Katherine McConnel

In 1900 Brisbane's Alcazar Press published a promotional history of Queensland entitled, *Queensland 1900: A narrative of her past together with biographies of her leading men.* Of particular interest is 'The history of Brisbane' chapter, in which an unidentified author passionately outlines the history of the city's development, its growth in 'importance' and concludes the paragraph with an interesting quandary:

> Four decades have seen Brisbane grow from a miserable dependency of New South Wales, absolutely neglected by the parent colony, and little heard of outside Australia at all, into a city of truly great dimensions, and the metropolis of what is freely admitted to be one of the finest ... . She was at the outset an outcast; her geographical position for years operated against her trade development and discounted her claims to importance. But in spite of her drawbacks, natural and manufactured, she steadily progressed until now ... and has a standing, which claims the respect of all her neighbours. With her lay the key to the Federal situation; both Victoria and New South Wales have at last admitted this.[1]

Such a declaration, that Brisbane had played a prominent part in the attainment of Australian federation, sits awkwardly with the fact that the returns for the Brisbane metropolitan district, from the 2 September 1899 federation referendum, presented a notable majority *against* federation.[2] Moreover, the Commonwealth Bill was defeated in all ten of Brisbane's electorates. 'The federal victory', the pro-federation *Brisbane courier* declared, 'was not a Brisbane victory'.[3] What then lay behind this reference to Brisbane as the key to the federal question?

As the author made no further mention of the federal issue in the Brisbane chapter, this paper examines aspects of the Brisbane federal campaign to shed light on the possible meaning of this puzzling statement. In conjunction with Brisbane's strong 'no' vote, this paper will concentrate largely on the anti-billites' campaign for the 1899 federation referendum.[4] Of particular interest will be the relationship between Queensland and New South Wales and the intersection of internal regional factors in Queensland with the federal question.

As the colony's capital city, the seat of government and administration and the main centre of population, Brisbane was as a consequence the focal centre of the federation issue in Queensland in 1899. The Anti-Convention Bill League was formed in Brisbane in April 1899 and organised an opposition which the *Brisbane courier* later acknowledged was 'perhaps the most determined ... that has ever marked a national movement'.[5] The metropolis too, was the chief centre for the Queensland Federation League from which 'the rays of federal light were sent out'.[6]

Prior to 1899 the general attitude to the federation movement of Brisbane and Queensland had been one of government hesitancy and public apathy. Such a stance had invited repeated criticism from the more active pro-federation southern colonies. G.B. Barton remarked that Queensland's absence from the Bathurst People's Convention in November 1896 was 'striking proof that she needs waking up on the subject of Federation'.[7] Significant public participation in the federal issue, however, was not awoken until less than three months before the September 1899 referendum. As a result, most Queenslanders had only a brief exposure to the arguments for and against federation. The brevity of the campaign provided some advantage to the anti-billite camp because evidence from the second referendum vote in New South Wales had suggested that an unsure voter was more likely to vote 'no'.[8] To promptly educate and influence the Queensland voter nevertheless became the crucial task of both the campaigns for and against federation.

1.1 Queensland Federation League rooms (old AMP Building), c.1899 (JOL)

Crucial to the promulgation of each side's arguments in the short Queensland federal campaign were Brisbane's principal newspapers, the pro-billite *Brisbane courier* and the anti-billite *Telegraph*. Utilising their wide circulation and influence, each paper attempted to counter opposing arguments, and to sway their readers through numerous articles and editorials on the federal topic and through detailed coverage of relevant public meetings. Both campaigns in general focused their attention on the wavering or undecided voter and, as a secondary approach, attempted to convert those who had decided.[9]

Confusion was one of the by-products of the abundant information presented to the people through the newspapers. The labour organ, the *Worker*, consequently remarked: 'To try and analyse the arguments dinned into our ears about the merits and demerits of Federation and anti-Federation is almost sufficient to drive one distracted'.[10] In light of this fact and because the provisions of the Commonwealth Bill were complex, and that expert opinion was so divided on the issues, additional strategies were put to use by both sides in an attempt to grab attention and to exert, hopefully, a decisive influence over the voter.

One such tactic which had a significant bearing on the referendum campaign was the anti-billites' appeal to local patriotism. 'Queensland for the Queenslanders' was a persistent and effective slogan for the anti-billites. However, it is important to note that the patriotic sentiment it contained had its strongest influence in the south-east corner of the colony, and particularly in Brisbane. At the core of this appeal to Queensland nationalism was antipathy towards the southern colonies, in particular New South Wales. This drew heavily on the unsatisfactory experience of NSW's administration in pre-separation days and on the bitterness surrounding Queensland's 1859 separation from the mother colony.[11] Self-government had not been easily won and an influential number of Queenslanders, old enough to remember the struggle for independence, were therefore unwilling to chance a second and more permanent arrangement of political integration. What was reiterated was Queensland's progress since separation, that, in short, she had 'moulded' her own destiny, could 'survive' on her own, and was no longer subject to the 'neglect' of a distant parliament.[12] The danger, it was forcefully argued, with the Commonwealth Bill and its introduction of a remote central government, was that it would negate this independence and progress and presented every possibility of Queensland becoming 'a mere appanage' of New South Wales or Victoria.[13] The weekly organ of the *Telegraph*, the *Week*, reminded its readers:

> For forty years Queensland has enjoyed that privilege [self-government], and with it has achieved both prestige and prosperity. ... The last generation fought for the right of local self-government, and achieved their desire on the 10th December 1859. Yet we are asked to resign all we gained, and voluntarily return to bondage on the 2nd September 1899.[14]

In Brisbane, John Robertson warned 'All those who remember the state of subservience under which we groaned before we obtained our present free constitution will hold back from consenting to our surrendering the position'.[15] A further aspect, highlighted in the argument which promoted the maintenance of independence, was the degree to which Queenslanders saw, and jealously guarded, their identity as a separate country within the continent of Australia. Defending one's birthright and nation became a familiar theme in the campaign against federation, as evocatively presented in a 'Patriotic Song' published in the *Week*:

Ye native youth of Queensland,
Who, true to noble birth,
Now form a mighty army,
Fight.
For altar and for hearth.

Your enemies are mighty.
In numbers, brass, and gold;
But rally to the standard.
Fight.
Your nation's flag to hold.

With you are right and freedom,
Your fathers gave them to you,
A great and blessed heirship,
Fight.
Ye stout of heart and true.

'Our cry is, No surrender!'
We natives of the soil,
Intend to be a nation;
Fight we will.
For Providence doth smile.

He is for our battalions.
He must be for the right.
For freedom and for justice;
Fight we shall and put
The aliens to flight.[16]

Beyond the considerable space allocated by the anti-billite press to articles and editorials maintaining and generating Queensland nationalism, what was more indicative of its strong influence was the vigorous efforts of the federalist camp to neutralise its impact. The central tenet of the federalist strategy was the promotion of Australian nationalism with its emphasis on the common heritage of most Australians and the apparent naturalness of sealing these bonds. This ideal was best encapsulated in the two key federalist slogans: 'One people, one destiny' and 'Unity is strength'. Such cries for a holy brotherhood of the colonies, however, served to further aggravate anti-billites' suspicion of southern plans to control the smaller colonies. A letter from F.T. Brentnall MLC to the *Week* argued:

> In what respect during 40 years has that colony [New South Wales] shown any generous friendliness to Queensland? .... We must not suspect our kind neighbours of seeking federation for the good it will do them. Oh no! They are imbued with lofty national sentiment, with broad generosity, they are inspired by a sublime idealism.[17]

Despite repeated attacks, Australian nationalism was largely an unassailable part of the federalist case. What is of particular interest was the federalist's secondary, though linked scheme, to rout Queensland nationalism through the manipulation of inter-regional tensions.

At the core of this federalist tactic was the provocative identification of Queensland nationalism as a sentiment peculiar to the south-east corner and more specifically as Queen Street parochialism. In this classification, the federalist's goal was to harness Northern and Central Queensland's strong and long existing antipathy to Brisbane. Resentment by these regions centred on Brisbane's dominance of the colony, maintained by the capital's location in the extreme south-east corner, the government's inefficient administration, and Brisbane's 'leech-like rapacity' in relation to public money.[18] Dissatisfaction had developed into a series of passionate but unsuccessful campaigns for the territorial separation of Queensland into three self-governing colonies. The repeated rejection of the demands for separation by a government numerically commanded by southerners was seen as Brisbane's self-interested maintenance of her economic and political dominance. With this in mind, the opposition to federation, projected through Queensland nationalism, was seen as a further plot by Brisbane to maintain her supremacy.

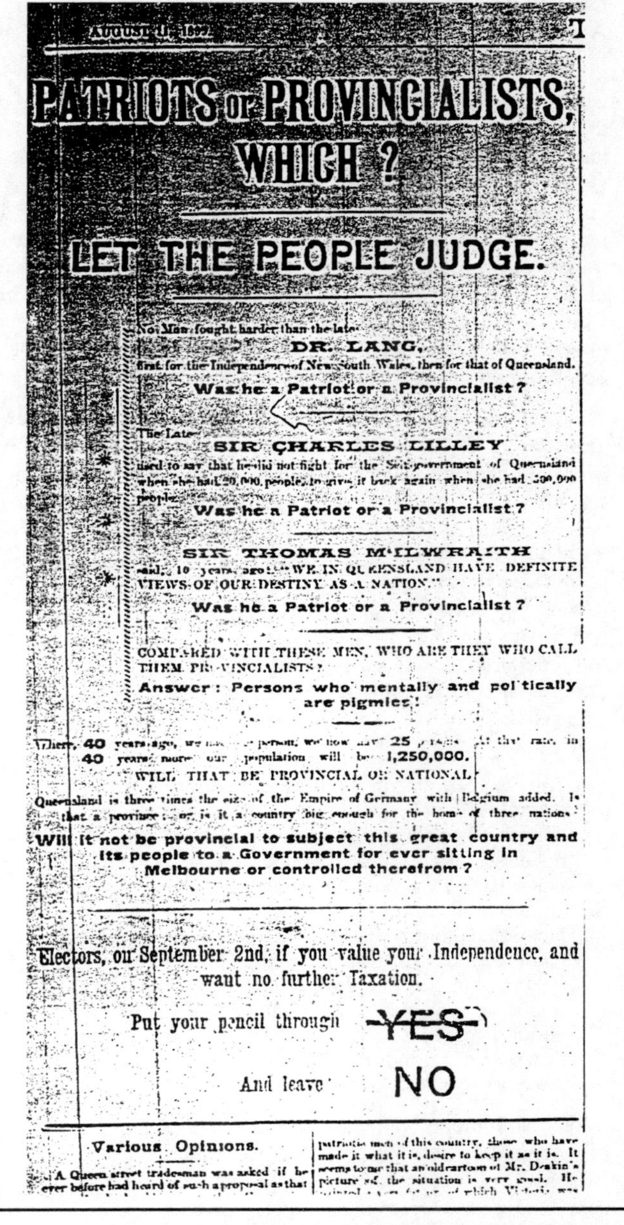

AUGUST 11, 1899.

PATRIOTS OR PROVINCIALISTS, WHICH ?

LET THE PEOPLE JUDGE.

No Man fought harder than the late

DR. LANG,

first for the Independence of New South Wales, then for that of Queensland.

Was he a Patriot or a Provincialist ?

The Late

SIR CHARLES LILLEY

used to say that he did not fight for the Self-government of Queensland when she had 20,000 people, to give it back again when she had 500,000 people.

Was he a Patriot or a Provincialist ?

SIR THOMAS M'ILWRAITH

said, 10 years ago: "WE IN QUEENSLAND HAVE DEFINITE VIEWS OF OUR DESTINY AS A NATION."

Was he a Patriot or a Provincialist ?

COMPARED WITH THESE MEN, WHO ARE THEY WHO CALL THEM PROVINCIALISTS ?

Answer : Persons who mentally and politically are pigmies !

Where, 40 years ago, we [illegible] person, we now have 25 persons. At that rate, in 40 years more our population will be 1,250,000.

WILL THAT BE PROVINCIAL OR NATIONAL ?

Queensland is three times the size of the Empire of Germany with Belgium added. Is that a province ; or is it a country big enough for the home of three nations ?

Will it not be provincial to subject this great country and its people to a Government for ever sitting in Melbourne or controlled therefrom ?

Electors, on September 2nd, if you value your Independence, and want no further Taxation,

Put your pencil through ~~YES~~

And leave NO

Various Opinions.

A Queen street tradesman was asked if he ever before had heard of such a proposal as that [illegible]

patriotic men of this country, those who have made it what it is, desire to keep it as it is. It seems to me that an old cartoon of Mr. Deakin's picture of the situation is very good. He [illegible]

1.2 'Patriots or Provincialists', the *Week* 11 Aug. 1899. Reproduced in the anti-billite press, this leaflet presented a passionate advocacy and summary of the Queensland Nationalists' argument against federation.

Federation was, as a consequence, promoted in the Central and more aggressively in the Northern regions, as a chance to attack the vested interests of Brisbane and as a means to confer many of the aims of separation.[19] Maryborough's *Wide Bay and Burnett news* concluded its federation campaign on 1 September by stressing to its electors 'that this is the last battle between Centralisation and Decentralisation. Federation offers Maryborough the last and only chance of to some extent checking the greed that has characterised the octopus of the South [Brisbane]'.[20] In the North, federalists flagrantly advanced the proposition that since the objectors to the federal bill resided mainly in Brisbane and that their ranks consisted of opponents of separation, this fact alone provided enough reason to vote for federation.[21] Further insight into the depth of antagonism between the North and the South was presented in the *Week*'s curt identification of the North's aim: 'And so the little game is to carry the bill by the northern vote ... southern Queensland cannot overlook that the Premier and the Treasurer are stirring up bitter feeling and strife in the north'.[22] Another aspect of the federalist platform in the North was an emphasis on the economic benefits that federation would provide and which were aligned to the separatists' cause.

Inter-colonial free trade had been one of the main objectives of the separation movement and a goal that federation would accomplish. The federalist argument declared that the main reason the South had opposed separation was Brisbane's desire to maintain its 'monopoly of the trade of North Queensland'.[23] Once free trade had been introduced by federation, this monopoly would be eliminated, as 'very little business will be done with the "brutal south"', thus removing the major reason for opposition to separation.[24] Apart from the separation question, the introduction of free trade was promoted as providing significant economic advantages for the North. An open Australian market would increase trade, create jobs and prosperity. The reduction of duties on imported goods would result in a reduction in the cost of living.[25] Against these potential benefits, the concerted opposition to federation on economic grounds in Brisbane again enticed the North to see that the South sought only to protect her own interests.

Dire predictions of the economic disaster that would befall Brisbane was the principal argument used by those who opposed federation. George Thorn MLA argued in parliament that 'was it not a deep-laid scheme to block the port of Moreton Bay? That was the whole thing in going into this scheme of federation – a deep-laid scheme to wipe out Brisbane'.[26] North Queensland in particular was charged repeatedly with threatening the primacy of Brisbane to 'get even'.[27] These propositions were continued into the anti-billites' post-referendum dissection. The North was denounced for her large majority for federation,[28] and more significantly for the crucial role that this majority played in Queensland's narrow 55.4 percent vote for federation:[29]

> The excess voting is in the northern district. It is not a vote for the bill; it is a vote for separation. It is impossible to believe that the Parliament of Queensland will pass an address to the Queen in favour of the Convention Bill in face of Saturday's voting. ... Southern Queensland, so deeply interested in maintaining the interests of the port of Brisbane, will never consent to being handed over to her enemies at the dictation of northern Queensland. ... Let the North go.[30]

Such arguments validated the contention of separationists and federalists that Brisbane opposed federation to protect her supremacy, however the major concern Brisbane had with the economic clauses of

The Week, 1 September 1899.

1.3 'Queensland Will Not Federate', the *Week*, 1 Sep. 1899, 24. Political cartoons were the major visual element of the print media in the late nineteenth century and were particularly popular for their ability to crystallise complex issues into a simple metaphor. In this cartoon the fable of Little Red Riding Hood was used to illustrate the potential and dangerous relationship between the other colonies and Queensland if federation was achieved.

the Commonwealth Bill was not development of the North, but the anticipated domination of trade by the larger southern colonies.

Brisbane was by far the largest commercial and industrial centre in Queensland, although her manufacturing industries were, in the late 1890s, still in their infancy and were being nurtured by protective customs tariff on imported goods. A significant core of the opposition to federation and its associated intercolonial free trade consisted of those who feared competition from the more established manufacturers in Sydney and Melbourne.[31] The main markets for Brisbane's boot and shoe, timber, leather, soap, candle, biscuit, jam, and clothing manufacturers were within Queensland itself and it was feared that the larger southern factories were 'keenly anxious … for the annexation of Queensland' so they could 'flood' Queensland with their surplus and cheaper products.[32]

More divided opposition came from Brisbane's merchants and shopkeepers. Merchants who traded predominantly within the colony feared the decline of Brisbane's prestige and the subsequent loss to Sydney of their trade. These anxieties received wide airing as page after page of Brisbane's newspapers was filled with assertions, counter-assertions and contradictory statistics on the economic question, all of which invariably created confusion in the mind of the voter.

To simplify their case, anti-billites, drawing heavily on anti-New South Wales sentiment, published vignettes and short interviews to personalise and emotively drive home their key points. A Queen Street tradesman was asked 'if he ever before had heard of such a proposal as that Queensland should accept the Convention Bill. 'Oh Yes.' he said, 'I have often heard of persons committing suicide. I see no difference between the proposal and taking a rope and hanging yourself. It is suicide'.[33]

1.4 'Chorus of Little Queen-street Prophets', Q 20 May 1899, 927. This cartoon presents an unflattering caricature of Brisbane's businessmen who opposed federation. Ridicule through the cartoon was a simple and effective tactic in discrediting an opponent's argument.

The *Telegraph* alarmingly summarised the economic issue on the 2 September, '... in short, if they vote "yes", it means "poverty, hunger and dirt"; if they vote "no", it means continued and increased prosperity'.[34]

In the volley of claim and counter claim the federalists 'guaranteed' that federation would not negatively affect Brisbane. Her place, the *Queenslander* asserted, 'will be a foremost one, and that its importance will increase as the years go by'.[35] As with the promotion of the federal cause in the North, federalists also stressed the 'material advantages' federation offered Brisbane. The opening up of an Australian market would increase trade and prosperity. 'There is money in union ... profit will outweigh loss' the *Courier* declared.[36] To further promote federation, advocates challenged the idea that Queensland would prosper well enough without federation:

> The man who was content to do well was stagnant and non-progressive. A blackfellow in his canoe thought he was doing well, but that was no reason why steamers should not be employed; a bullock-dray 'did well', but they did not block employment of a train; it was not a question of 'How are we doing' or ' We are doing well', but 'Can we do better?'[37]

THE FEDERAL SITUATION UP NORTH.

SOUTHERN BILL: "*Well, I must be going. Are you coming with me?*"

NORTHERN ANTIBILL: "*You only want to rob me.*"

S. B.: "*No I don't.*"

N. A.: "*That proves you do, 'cause you never speak the truth.*"

S. B.: "*All right—I do then.*"

N. A.: "*There! I* KNEW *I'd make you admit it!*"

1.5 'The Federal Situation up North', the *Bulletin*, 26 Aug. 1899. This caricature of Queensland as a little hillbilly boy was employed regularly by the *Bulletin*. The simplicity of Queenslanders expressed in this caricature was strenuously challenged by anti-billites.

The aggregate of this ongoing barrage of arguments was the intensification of animosity between the opposing camps. On one level this was signified by the use of war terminology by the press, whereby the referendum vote was referred to as the federal 'conflict' or 'battle' and in which 'the enemy' 'took the field' with 'weapons' and 'wounds' were sustained.[38] On another front, the premier, James Dickson, received a threatening letter in which the author declared that if federation was achieved, 'I shall sout [shoot] you'.[39] The most overt expression of hostility occurred at the numerous public meetings on the subject. Heckling, flying objects and fights became a regular feature of these meetings, and at its most extreme prevented the speaker from finishing his speech. More commonly, the interference was temporary and on occasions humorous. An open-air meeting was held at noon at the gates of the Botanic Gardens on Edward Street, Brisbane, which attracted working men from the surrounding foundries. The *Courier* reported:

> The audience was generally attentive, although at times three or four 'fuddled' persons would persist in displaying their ignorance, and insulting those who went to listen and not annoy. Some one or more persons threw several handfuls of shot from Smellie and Co's upstairs windows and reduced the firm's stock by several pounds, but this by no means disturbed the proceedings, although it must be confessed it was an element of danger.[40]

More spirited agitation took place at the venues which presented prominent federalists from NSW and Victoria. At crucial times in the campaign speaking tours by these southern men, such as Alfred Deakin and Edmund Barton would, it was believed, win more votes than all the printer's ink in town.[41] In Brisbane, the stronghold of Queensland nationalism, the importation of these 'foreign devils' fuelled the anti-billites' case against federation.[42] First it was seen as a clear admission of weakness of the federal cause and second as a sly tactic to brainwash the voter:

> Who brings these imported speakers to Queensland? The federalists who are trembling lest the patriotic vote of Queensland should be too strong for them. Who are these cowards? ... men who rely on the good sense and good faith of their fellow colonists. Or the traitors who bring their borrowed talk from abroad to help us form opinions and learn to vote ... [and] to beguile us with platform clap trap into voting against our interests and our liberty. ... The voters of Queensland must throw back in their faces the lie of these slanderers and traitors.[43]

The physical attack on Barton on the eve of the referendum by those described as 'a mob of anti-billites [who] inveighed against Southern invaders',[44] illustrates the height of tension attained during the federation campaign particularly in Brisbane.[45]

Despite the anti-billites' repeated criticism of NSW, it is inaccurate to assert that relations with Queensland were so strained. Allegations of prior neglect and domination masked the reality that Queensland in the late 1890s had a closer relationship with NSW than any other colony. Jenkins compared the relationship to that of two brothers, in which Queensland, the younger brother, acknowledged the superior achievements of the elder colony yet challenged it in order to establish equality and independence. Discord was a by-product of this challenge.[46] On the federal issue there was agreement, at least politically, that NSW and Queensland should work together as their interests were inseparable. Neither colony therefore felt that they could enter a federation without the other. They must, as Barton stated, 'row in one boat as regards Federation'.[47] This compact drew criticism from the Melbourne-based journal, the *Review of reviews*. Queensland, it argued, had managed to shift the centre of political gravity with regard to federation, because she made everything depend on a colony that had taken no part in framing the Commonwealth Bill.[48] The interconnection between NSW and Queensland was evident in the acknowledged belief that the acceptance of federation, at NSW's second referendum, would impact positively on the federal chances in Queensland. Moreover, the success of federation in Queensland would provide the mother colony with her 'best ally' in matters where she might differ from her southern neighbours, namely, Victoria.[49] That colony also stressed the importance of Queensland coming in for its own reasons, and for the influence it would have on the federal cause in Western Australia. It is therefore quite apparent that Queenslanders and the other colonies were aware of the commanding card Queensland held in the game of federation. Yet it is only the scornful anti-Brisbane logic of Sydney's *Bulletin* which claimed that Queensland's apparent influence in the federal issue was reduced down to Brisbane and then further down to the anti-federal *Telegraph* and its owner George Cowlishaw:

> in admiration of the eternally-multiplying Queensland it follows that Bananaland should boss the whole of the southern hemisphere; that Brisbane should boss the possessions of Bananaland, and Brisbane itself should be bossed by the cultural gang that runs the COWLIGRAPH.[50]

What role then did Brisbane play in the attainment of Australian federation? Brisbane's concentration of population and the strength of her influence as the capital of the colony clearly made a concerted campaign a necessity for the federation foes. Moreover, Brisbane's avowed opposition to the Commonwealth Bill forced the federalists to focus on Brisbane. The *Telegraph* noted that it was in the metropolitan district that the federalists 'made their most strenuous efforts; therein they spent their money, they poured out their newspaper and platform advocacy, and to it brought their southern contingents to fight for them; all this was done and yet they lost'.[51] The strength of the anti-billites' campaign in Brisbane was centred around a powerful suspicion of the southern colonies 'base and mercenary purpose' in advancing federation.[52] The fear that NSW and Victoria would politically and economically dominate Queensland in an Australian federation was aggressively advanced, and countered by Queensland nationalism. The results of the Brisbane referendum vote displayed the strength of the opposition, with Brisbane 'rejecting the Bill emphatically' by 2 to 1 votes against.[53] The pre-vote estimates, however, had predicted that Brisbane would produce a 4 to 1 vote against federation.[54] Such a disparity does then indicate that the federalists' campaign did, in part, erode the strength of Queensland nationalism, the fear of economic ruination and thus the 'No' vote. This, however, does not wholly support the proposition that Brisbane was the key to the federal issue. The pro-federation *Courier* confirmed this as it claimed that it was not in Brisbane 'that the battle was to be fought. The whole of Queensland was the field'.[55]

Activism in the Northern and Central districts was crucial to the federalists' cause in Queensland. Within this campaign a strong predilection, fanned by 'Federal propaganda', was hostility to Brisbane.[56] Through the aggravation of existing inter-regional tensions, federalists actively encouraged an affinity between separation and federation in their promotion of the Commonwealth Bill. Despite the clearly negative connotations of this approach, it can, nevertheless, be advanced that Brisbane played a contributing role in the acceptance of federation. The North, and to a lesser extent the Centre, produced a decisive 'yes' vote attracted by the post-federation economic advantages and to avenge the neglect and exploitation of the 'ruling gang in Brisbane'.[57] This solid support for federation provided the fundamental counter vote to the hostile South and, in particular, Brisbane returns. Qualification, however, is necessary.

Brisbane's perceptible role was arguably confined to the acceptance of the Commonwealth Bill by the majority of Queenslanders and not in the attainment of federation Australia-wide. Outside Queensland the link between Brisbane and her crucial role in federation becomes more tenuous. Certainly the fact that Queensland's referendum vote was taken after federation had been accepted by the southern colonies did place greater significance on the Queensland vote. The desire of these colonies to have the federal compact achieved does not, however, imply the crucial role of Brisbane. Arguably, the concerted effort by NSW to affirm brotherly relations and to ameliorate Brisbane's economic fears did highlight the existence of a significant lynchpin between Brisbane and Sydney and federation. Alternatively though, much of the Sydney *Bulletin*'s pro-federation coverage of the Queensland campaign consisted of anti-Brisbane sentiment. Moreover, NSW had solidly accepted federation and was unlikely to withdraw if Queensland failed to join. On the Western Australian front a federation victory in Queensland was seen primarily for its run-on effect, that of enhancing the federal chances of success in the west.

In this context it could be argued that the unidentified author who maintained that Brisbane was the key to federation, saw it as a general signifier of Queensland as a whole. It consequently becomes apparent that the true meaning of the author's claim that Brisbane held 'the key to the Federal situation' will continue to remain in the realm of conjecture. No definitive explanation seems to sufficiently justify this statement. While Brisbane was unmistakably hostile to federation from the beginning of the campaign to well after the referendum, she continued to prioritise herself above the rest of Queensland. It is possible that within the wordy and fiery efforts to maintain this prior position the author saw Brisbane playing a prominent role. On referendum day, however, Queensland answered the appeal of Australian union, and Brisbane, as the *Bulletin* saw it, 'ran up against … ordinary fate'.[58]

02 Federation
The view from the Chief Secretary's Department
Joanne Scott

The centenary of Australia's federation has encouraged a wealth of new studies on the sometimes tortuous series of negotiations which led to the formation of the Commonwealth of Australia; on the key political figures who participated in those negotiations; on the economic, social and cultural contexts against which the Australian colonies adopted a federal system of government; and on the consequences of federation both for Australians and for those individuals who were excluded from the definition of Australian citizenship.

This chapter seeks to enhance our understanding of those themes and of the significance of federation in citizens' daily lives by exploring the impact of federation on a specific group of Queenslanders – the public servants who were employed in the Chief Secretary's Department and their political masters. After providing an outline of the roles of the Chief Secretary's Department in the years prior to 1901, it details some of the effects of federation on the staff, the work and the power associated with the Department. Given the role of senior colonial politicians in the federation process as well as the particular responsibilities of the Chief Secretary's head office and sub-departments, it seems that the officials within this branch of the public service in particular should have been involved in the negotiations that culminated in federation and affected by its declaration. By some measures that is certainly true.

Yet, an examination of the correspondence generated within the Chief Secretary's head office and the changes which occurred in that office in the years immediately before and after federation suggests that, in terms of the day-to-day lives of Queensland public servants, we need to be careful not to overestimate the impact of federation. So, in addition to acknowledging the effects of federation on the Chief Secretary's Department, this chapter also situates federation within the context of the range of activities undertaken by the Chief Secretary and his staff in the last years of the nineteenth and the first years of the twentieth centuries.

2.1 Samuel Griffith in later life (JOL)

The Chief Secretary's Department before 1901

Premier Samuel Griffith created the position of Chief Secretary in Queensland in 1886 in order to reduce the workload associated with the post of Colonial Secretary. By the mid-1880s, the Colonial Secretary's Department had 'supervision of an immense number of things inside the colony' and was also responsible for Queensland's external relations.[2] As Griffith explained, 'The work attached to the office of Colonial Secretary, which was held by myself, was found more than I could attend to in addition to other matters more particularly connected with my position as head of the Government'.[3] He detailed his new responsibilities as Chief Secretary:

> Legislation, defence, foreign correspondence, immigration, commissions and other instruments under the Great Seal of the Colony; and the correspondence with His Excellency the Governor, the Judges of the Supreme Court, the President and Clerk of the Legislative Council, the Speaker and Clerk of the Legislative Assembly, the consuls of foreign States, naval and military authorities, the Secretaries of Colonial Governments, the Agent-General, the heads of the several Churches, and the Government Resident at Thursday Island; and is further charged, in conjunction with the Colonial Secretary, with the control of such other matters attached to the Colonial Secretary's Department as may from time to time be found expedient.[4]

Initially the Chief Secretary's staff operated as a sub-section within the Colonial Secretary's and then the Home Secretary's Office. In mid-1898 a separate Chief Secretary's Department was created. Explaining this decision to parliament, the Chief Secretary and first Queensland-born premier, Thomas Byrnes, emphasised the importance of the work undertaken by his staff. He declared that: 'There had been a large increase in the amount of foreign correspondence; defence matters occupied a great deal of time, and there was a general supervision in the department over legislation and over practically the whole course of administration'.[5] While these claims can be substantiated, the Premier's next statement does not appear to be supported by available evidence. According to Byrnes, 'There have been many things added to the Chief Secretary's Department that have been taken from other departments'.[6]

2.2 Thomas Joseph Byrnes (JOL)

In 1898, however, just five sub-departments reported to the Chief Secretary – the Agent-General, Immigration, Government Vessels, Land and Marine Defence, and Quarantine; the last was transferred to the Home Secretary in 1900. Nearly 700 staff worked within the sub-departments, the great majority in Land and Marine Defence. Following the administrative separation of the Home and Chief Secretary's head offices, the latter expanded to include ten employees: the Under Secretary, chief clerk, record clerk and accountant, shorthand writer and clerk, correspondence clerk, three additional clerks and two messengers.

In the nineteenth century, the power of the Chief Secretary and his staff derived from two key factors. First, the Chief Secretary usually, although not always, held the post of Premier or Prime Minister of Queensland. Under Secretary Henry Dutton commented in 1899 that 'any question of general policy is referred to the Chief Secretary's Department, which, being presided over by the Prime Minister, must necessarily act as a controlling medium in all important business for which the Head of the Government is responsible'. He added that 'all legislation and everything connected with the administration of the Public Service as a whole must be conducted through this office'.[7]

The other major source of power for the Chief Secretary's Department before 1901 derived from its focus on external affairs, including defence and immigration. The last decades of the nineteenth century witnessed increasing inter-colonial and imperial negotiations over numerous issues including the future of New Guinea, joint defence arrangements and, of course, federation itself. Negotiations over defence included the 1887 London Conference at which Britain and the Australian colonies discussed the British navy's Australasian Squadron and cooperative efforts for the defence of Thursday Island and King George Sound. These topics recurred at subsequent inter-colonial conferences during the 1890s and in correspondence among the colonial premiers. Queensland also entered discussions about the formation of a single army for the Australian colonies.

Negotiating federation

On 1 January 1901 the Commonwealth of Australia was proclaimed. The lead-up to the creation of a federated Australia had certainly generated additional work for the Chief Secretary and his head office. As the section of Queensland's administration responsible for extra-colonial relations, the office played a key role in Queensland's negotiations with the other Australian colonies, as well as intervening in and overseeing Queensland's preparations for federation. Surviving records from the Chief Secretary's Department include details of Queensland's involvement in the inter-colonial conferences of the 1890s and the London conference of 1900, and material on the Australasian Federation Enabling Bill (Queensland) of 1899 and the Commonwealth Bill of 1900. They also include correspondence among colonial politicians over such issues as the numbers of members from each colony in the future federal House of Representatives and the appropriate date for the first federal elections.

2.3 Robert Philp (JOL)

Premier Robert Philp expressed concerns over the latter subject when the Premier of Victoria, Allan McLean, advocated federal elections in 1900. Philp responded:

> I am still of opinion that to hurry on the Elections for the time suggested will result in very great confusion. I am afraid that when we are actually engaged in the work of establishing the Commonwealth, we shall find it something very different from a matter of ordinary departmental administration within a Colony, and we must take into account not only the number of things that must be done before the Elections can be held, but the vast size of some of the Colonies, whose most remote constituencies must receive long notice of the dates fixed upon in order that proper arrangements may be made for polling.[8]

Negotiations concerning federation, however, constituted only one of the many roles undertaken by the Chief Secretary's head office prior to 1 January 1901. In July 1898, for example, the month in which the office was established as a separate entity, the subjects raised in inwards and outwards correspondence included defence, immigration, purchase of goods overseas, government vessels, and negotiations with other colonies. In addition there were requests for employment, petitions for wage increases, and correspondence associated with the creation, furnishing and administration of the new department. Other letters discussed such diverse issues as a proposed Harbour Board Bill; the salaries of medical doctors who provided services to the government; the mail service between Barcaldine and Blackall; the railway freight charged for the carriage of homing pigeons; the Queensland education system including the future of the Brisbane Technical College; a proposed tramway in Geraldton; methods for destroying cattle ticks; an exhibition by the Toowoomba branch of the Royal Agricultural Society of Queensland; and a missing persons enquiry. In the same month, Premier Byrnes received deputations on the Early Closing campaign, conditions in the sugar industry, the political enfranchisement of women, the conduct of work by public departments on Sundays, and the principle of 'one man, one vote'. In mid-July Dutton wrote to an individual who had requested a meeting with the Chief Secretary: 'Mr Byrnes' time is so fully occupied with pressing Official business that he is unable to grant the desired interview at present'.[9]

2.4 Hugh Nelson (JOL)

The Chief Secretary's correspondence for the 1890s indicates that federation was not always a priority during that decade. Although Griffith played a major role in the federation movement during the early 1890s, his enthusiasm was not shared by all of his successors. Premier Hugh Nelson was at best hesitant about federation, notwithstanding an 1894 letter in which he expressed 'great gratification' at NSW's decision to 'again take a leading part in the movement for Australian federation'.[10] Nelson's successor, T.J. Byrnes, believed that it would be premature for the colony to enter a federated Australia. The Queensland government's attendance at the various federal conventions was patchy – delegates attended the 1890 and 1891 conventions, but the colony did not send any representatives to the 1893 and 1897-98 meetings. Only when James Dickson assumed the premiership in October 1898 did Queensland again have a head of government who actively supported federation. Dickson attended the 1899 Premiers' Conference at which final details about federation were negotiated, and in May 1899 he introduced a bill to enable a referendum on his colony's entry to federation. In September Queensland recorded the narrowest 'yes' margin of any Australian colony on the issue.

While some of the activity in the Chief Secretary's office in relation to federation concerned policy development and decisions, particularly in the years immediately prior to federation, there were also more mundane matters to consider. For example, staff worked to ensure the efficient communication of decisions among interested parties. In 1900 Dickson, then Chief Secretary but no longer Premier, attended the London conference on federation, and correspondence flowed between the Chief Secretary's office and London. From late 1899 the office had been generating material for two government ministers, with the separation of the posts of Premier and Chief Secretary. Robert Philp was Premier and Dickson was Chief Secretary. The two posts were recombined from early 1901.

2.5 James Dickson (JOL)

As well as the major issues surrounding Queensland's participation in the federation of the Australian colonies, the Chief Secretary's office also dealt with minor details, notably those relating to the occasion of federation itself. There was correspondence about the celebrations in Brisbane and other parts of Queensland. Arrangements were made to ensure the availability of James Brunton Stephens' federation poem in north Queensland to coincide with its publication in other parts of Australia. One of the best known of Australia's nineteenth century poets and playwrights, Brunton Stephens was a senior public servant in the Chief Secretary's office.

In the months immediately prior to federation, the office received inquiries from individuals hoping to be invited to attend the celebrations in Sydney. Philp, apparently somewhat exasperated by this issue, wrote to the NSW Premier, William Lyne, in November 1900:

> I shall esteem it a great favour if you will furnish me with such information as it may be possible at this stage to communicate with regard to the invitations to be issued to prominent men in this Colony to be present at the ceremonial inauguration of the Commonwealth at Sydney ... I am troubling you with this request because ... numerous inquiries on the subject are being addressed to me by persons who might presumably be included in the arrangements.[11]

Beyond 1 January

Given its emphasis on external relations, the Chief Secretary's Department faced a loss of powers and responsibilities after the first of January. In March 1901, for example, defence was transferred to the federal government. When the Public Service Board reviewed the operations of the Chief Secretary's office later that year, it commented that

> The business with the Land and Marine Defence Forces was until March last under the supervision and control of the Chief Secretary, and entailed a very considerable amount of work upon the Staff of this Department; but in that month the Defence Force was taken over entirely by the Commonwealth Government, and although a certain amount of the correspondence must necessarily pass between the Chief Secretary and the Federal Government for some time yet the work has materially decreased.[12]

Federation resulted in a dramatic decline in the number of staff who reported to the Chief Secretary. In 1900, he had controlled 856 staff; by 1903 there were just eighty. Staff numbers continued to decline until 1905, when they reached a low of sixty-three, despite the inclusion that year of the Auditor-General/Audit office and the Public Service Board within the Chief Secretary's portfolio.

Federation also prompted some re-evaluation of the Queensland public service. Three months before the inauguration of the Commonwealth and under instructions from the Premier, Under Secretary Dutton invited the public service heads of Queensland's other ministerial departments to attend a confidential meeting. The purpose of the meeting was to discuss possible amendments to the Public Service Act. Dutton explained that two impending events had prompted the meeting: 'The approaching expiration by effluxion of time of the term of office of the Public Service Board and ... the transfer, consequent upon the Establishment of the Commonwealth of Australia, of a large number of Public Servants to the control of the Federal Executive'.[13]

While federation resulted in the loss of some functions from the Chief Secretary's office, it also created a new tier of inter-governmental relations. The office became a focal point for Queensland's relations with the federal government and other state governments of Australia. Historian Denis Murphy refers to 'much "sorting out" of Commonwealth-state relations during the first decade of the twentieth century'.[14] That 'sorting out' can be traced through correspondence in the Chief Secretary's office. Queensland's response to federation and its relations with the new Commonwealth government were not always congenial. Much early tension centred on the use of Pacific Islanders in Queensland's sugar industry and the viability of that industry after the deportation of most Pacific Islanders from Australia under the federal government's 1901 Pacific Island Labourers Act.

Extensive correspondence generated from Premier Philp on the Act and its implications for Queensland included, in December 1901, one of the longest letters ever to come out of the Chief Secretary's office. Across eighteen pages, Philp complained to Australian Prime Minister Edmund Barton that 'Queensland had been singled out for summary correction at the very earliest possible moment after the power of the State to regulate entirely its own industries has passed into the hands of the Commonwealth Government'. Philp described the Act as 'revolutionary' and criticised Barton's ideas for ensuring the future of the sugar industry.[15] He also tried to persuade Queensland's Lieutenant Governor, Samuel Griffith, to request the Governor-General of Australia to reserve the Bill, to give the Queensland government time to appeal to His Majesty against the legislation. Later premiers adopted a more conciliatory approach, accepting the commonwealth government's power to repatriate Pacific Islanders and seeking to ensure federal assistance with that process.

Business as usual

Federation had a dramatic impact on the Chief Secretary's Department in terms of the transfer of staff and some roles to the new Commonwealth. As early as January 1901 it is possible to trace the emergence of new relationships as the Chief Secretary's range of correspondents expanded to include federal authorities. One of the earliest topics of discussion between Premier Philp and Australian Prime Minister Barton was, sadly, the death of James Dickson, who had accepted a post in Barton's government. On 10 January Barton sent a telegram to Philp about arrangements for Dickson's funeral. The following day, Philp wrote to Barton:

> On behalf of this State, I gratefully acknowledge your message of sympathy with the people, Parliament and Government of Queensland in the loss they have sustained by the death of the late Chief Secretary Sir James Dickson, who had so recently become your colleague as a Member of the Government of the Commonwealth in which capacity I have no doubt that his services would have secured him the same appreciative recognition which he had long enjoyed here as a statesman of the first importance in his Colony.[16]

Philp arranged for Andrew Wilson, a member of the Queensland Legislative Council, to represent the commonwealth government at the funeral and organised, at Barton's request, a wreath with 'a suitable inscription'.

While federation had a major effect on the Chief Secretary's office, in some respects change was only partial. Establishment of the commonwealth did not, for example, result in the Chief Secretary's Department eschewing all of its 'external' functions. Queensland retained its Agent-General's office in London and continued its involvement in immigration, although it now had to abide by

Commonwealth immigration laws and regulations. The Queensland parliament discussed the future of the Agent-General in 1902, with Philp declaring that 'there was an immense amount of work to be done' by the Agent-General and that Queensland would require a representative in London so long as the commonwealth did not appoint an Agent-General for Australia.[17]

2.6 Dickson's funeral procession at All Saints Church, Wickham Terrace (JOL)

The federation of the Australian colonies did not cause a noticeable decrease in the work of the Agent-General's office. Horace Tozer was Agent-General from 1898 to 1909. His annual reports, which journalist and historian Clem Lack described as 'voluminous masterpieces of ponderous prolixity', reveal the extraordinary quantity of work conducted in his office.[18] In 1902, for example, Tozer had a staff of thirteen, three more than the Chief Secretary's head office. In that year, the Agent-General's office received 12,250 letters and telegrams and despatched 34,300 items of 'printed matter and parcels' and more than 13,000 letters. Tozer commented that 'These are exclusive of some thousands of letters of a semi-public character written by my own hand'. He added that the recent installation of a telephone meant that 'some work hitherto appearing in correspondence is now transacted by telephone, which contributes largely to the convenience of the public, and manifestly to the unrecorded work of the Department'.[19]

The value of an overseas representative for Queensland was questioned in later years. In 1910, for example, parliamentarian Joe Lesina queried the need for a state representative in Britain, given that Queensland was now part of a federated Australia. Then Premier William Kidston replied that the Agent-General's staff undertook 'a great deal of valuable work', referred specifically to their duties in relation to immigration and indents, and asserted that in addition to its commercial roles, the office 'contributed to the dignity of the State'.[20] One hundred years after federation, Queensland maintains its representative in London.

In assessing the effect of federation on the Chief Secretary's office, it is also important to recognise that some of the significant changes to the staffing and work of that office in the years immediately prior to and following January 1901 were not related to the creation of the commonwealth. A noticeable alteration in staffing early in the twentieth century which had no connection with federation, for example, was the employment of women in the Chief Secretary's office beyond the role of 'office keeper'. By late 1901, three women – Mrs B.M.Cole, Miss Emily Thynne and Miss Maud Barclay – were working for the Chief Secretary as typists. The other major changes in staff roles early in the new century derived from the deaths of the two senior public servants in the head office – Henry Dutton and James Brunton Stephens.

Other aspects of work in the office acknowledged the existence of the commonwealth but the work itself represented a continuation of earlier functions. Protocol duties, for example, were a traditional part of the work undertaken by the Chief Secretary's staff. In 1901 those duties expanded to include protocol issues relating to such matters as whether federal or state government ministers would have precedence at functions in Queensland.

Conclusion

The negotiations which led to the federation of the Australian colonies, the celebrations which marked the establishment of the commonwealth on 1 January 1901, and the creation of a new tier of inter-governmental relations in this country all affected the Chief Secretary's Department. The correspondence of the Chief Secretary's head office reveals the contribution of that office to the process of federation as well as the consequences of federation for the Chief Secretary and his staff. Although the Department lost some of its power and employees to the commonwealth, the Chief Secretary and his senior public servants gained new responsibilities as they 'sorted out' relations between the federal and Queensland governments. We should be careful, though, not to overstate the impact of federation. Many of the nineteenth century roles of the Chief Secretary's Department continued beyond 1901 and federation was only one of the factors which influenced the work of the Chief Secretary and his staff.

03 Queensland local government in the federation decade

John Laverty

In many respects the federation decade represents a turning point in the development of local government in Queensland. The implementation of the recommendations of the Report of the 1896 Royal Commission on Local Government through the Health Act of 1900 and the Local Authorities Act of 1902 consolidated and extended the local government system.[1] The economic depression of the early 1890s led to vital changes in the financial arrangements of local authorities, especially those of the municipalities of Brisbane and South Brisbane, and the concept of a greater Brisbane was firmly placed in the public arena.

The Royal Commission on Local Government of 1896 was the most significant event in the development of local government in Queensland until the enactment of the City of Brisbane Act in 1924. It involved a comprehensive and thorough investigation of local government law and practice in the colony by its twenty-one members 'who had an intimate knowledge of the strengths, weaknesses, problems and needs of local government throughout the Colony'.[2] They were also able in their deliberations to draw on the knowledge and experience of the Home Secretary's Department, which oversaw the operation of local government in the colony, and on the opinions and suggestions of the many local authorities that made submissions to the commission. The commission obviously had a special insight into the operation of local government in the Brisbane metropolitan area since both William H.G. Marshall, Town Clerk of the Municipality of Brisbane and Alderman William Stephens of South Brisbane were members of the commission. Marshall also gave extensive evidence to the commission. In putting its recommendations into legal form, the commission was able to rely on the services of the parliamentary draftsman, John L. Woolcock.

The Local Government Act of 1878 and the Divisional Boards Act of 1879 created twin systems of local government. The Local Government Act operated in urban areas and their closely settled hinterlands while the more basic divisional boards legislation was compulsorily applied to the 'rural' areas of the colony. But as the population increased and the economy expanded, the divisional boards legislation increasingly borrowed provisions from the Local Government acts. Consequently by 1890 the nature and functions of divisional boards resembled those of municipal councils. Not surprisingly therefore, the Royal Commission recommended that the two systems of local government be combined into a single system of 'towns' and 'shires'. The system was extended to include 'cities' by the Local Authorities Act of 1902. This consolidation of the state's local authorities laid down a legal framework for a comprehensive network of local government. Apart from the City of Brisbane Act of 1924, local government law during the next thirty years was largely an extension of the 1902 act.

This reform was of particular importance in the Brisbane metropolitan area where there was a disparate mosaic of municipalities, shires and divisional boards, each required to exercise essentially the same functions and to provide much the same services. Under the new arrangements the system of local authorities in the metropolitan area was soon adjusted to more fully reflect the needs of the communities involved. The Municipality of Brisbane was up-graded to the status of a city by the Local Authorities Act of 1902 while the Borough of South Brisbane and the Shire of Sandgate were designated towns. The remaining metropolitan local authorities became shires under this legislation. Exercising the discretionary power granted by the act, the government subsequently adjusted the status of the local authorities in the metropolitan area to urban realities. In 1903 South Brisbane was proclaimed a city and the inner city local authorities of Toowong, Ithaca, Windsor and Hamilton were given the status of towns. Apart from the reconstitution of the bayside shire of Wynnum as a town in 1912, the metropolitan system of local authorities was not again altered until the advent of Greater Brisbane in 1925.

The Royal Commission's approval of a ratepayer franchise and plural voting in local government elections and its opposition to granting the vote to Aborigines, South Sea Islanders and Asians was enshrined in the Local Authorities Act of 1902 which continued the ratepayer franchise and the practice of plural voting, and restricted voting to adult natural-born or naturalised ratepayers. However, the future direction of franchise reforms was signalled by Labor members of parliament who unsuccessfully pressed for the introduction of an adult franchise in local government elections or, at least, for the adoption of the principle of one ratepayer one vote. In an attempt to solve the problem of 'hung' councils over the election of the mayor or chairman, James Tolmie unsuccessfully moved an amendment to the Local Authorities Bill in 1902 for the mayor or chairman to be elected directly by the electors.[3] This anticipated yet another of the Labor Party's local government electoral reforms of 1920 which provided for the adult franchise, 'one man one vote', the election of the mayor or chairman directly by the electors and triennial local government elections.[4]

Convinced that local authorities had exercised the functions and powers available to them, the Royal Commission concluded 'that in many important directions further powers could be assigned to them with manifest advantage to the good government of the colony'.[5] Not surprisingly the commission recommended a substantial extension of their existing powers, including wider control over roads; power to fix the level of roads; ample power to regulate land and water traffic; power to beautify areas under their control; exclusive control over pounds and impounding; control over foreshores; power to establish and control cemeteries; ample power to eradicate noxious weeds and to destroy pests; and authority to control hawkers and peddlers in their areas. In recognition of their increasing maturity, the commission also recommended that local authorities be given power to construct and control tramways; to establish and maintain gas and electricity undertakings and to conserve and supply hydraulic and other forms of power.

The commission also recommended that local authorities be granted greater powers to preserve public health, including power to punish those selling adulterated drugs and articles unfit for human consumption, and to check the spread of stock diseases. Authority for local bodies to become involved in food preservation by providing cold storage and chilling works for meat and farm produce and to supervise weights and measures was also recommended. The commission obviously concluded that local authorities should be concerned with cultural and social matters recommending that they be given the power to provide, control, or contribute towards the maintenance of libraries, technical schools, art galleries, reading rooms, schools of arts, museums and other institutions of similar character and authority to assist institutions, societies or organisations for the relief of distress and to licence and control theatres and places of amusement. In order to clarify the legal position of local authorities, the commission recommended that they should be given the power to compromise breaches of contract and actions at law and to protect against frivolous claims for damages due to the negligence of the council or its servants. They were also given the right to claim the assistance of the police in the execution of local government legislation.

Most of the health powers recommended by the commission were subsequently granted to local authorities by the Health Act of 1900 and kindred legislation. One of the most significant changes introduced by this act was the replacement of the Central Board of Health by a Commissioner of Health as the overseer of public health in Queensland, and the establishment of a bona-fide state health department.[6] Local authorities were responsible to the health commissioner for most aspects of public health in their areas, including the control of infectious diseases, sanitation, drainage and sewerage, prevention of nuisances, regulation of lodging-houses and offensive trades, infant life protection, control of the adulteration of food and drugs, regulation of the carriage, storage, distribution, inspection and sale of perishable foods and the supervision of weights and measures.

However, since the government concluded that few local authorities would be likely to provide cold storage and chilling facilities, these were left under the control of the Live Stock and Meat Export and Dairy Encouragement acts. The South Brisbane City Council subsequently established extensive cold stores under this legislation in conjunction with Geddes, Birt & Company at Musgrave

Wharf on the South Brisbane reach of the Brisbane River. Since experience had shown that local authorities were not able to effectively control dairies or supervise the production of milk products, the existing arrangements were continued until the responsibility for the supervision of the dairying industry was transferred to a government department by the Dairy Produce Act of 1904. Subsequent health and kindred legislation for more than two decades was essentially an extension of the principles of the 1900 act with, in some cases, responsibility for aspects of public health being transferred from local authorities to government departments or agencies.

Some of the new provisions of the Local Authorities Act of 1902 were inoperative in Brisbane. For example, the power of local authorities to establish and maintain gas and electricity undertakings could not be exercised because gas supply was already in the hands of the Brisbane and South Brisbane gas companies, and the Brisbane Electric Supply Company had been granted an order-in-council under the Electric Light & Power Act of 1896 to supply electricity in the city, even though the Brisbane Municipal Council had also applied for the franchise. Similarly, the Metropolitan Tramway & Investment Company Limited had been granted the right to establish and operate tramways in Brisbane under the Tramways Act of 1882 despite the attempts of the Brisbane Municipal Council to secure an order-in-council to do so. It was not until 1918 that suburban local authorities began distributing electricity purchased from the City Electric Light Company in their areas, and not until 1930 that the Brisbane City Council began generating significant amounts electricity for other than tramway purposes. Tramways were not placed under the control of the Tramway Trust until 1922. They were subsequently transferred to the control of the Brisbane City Council at the end of 1925.

The city's cemeteries and some of its parks remained under the control of government appointed trusts for many years. The Brisbane Traffic Act of 1895 transferred the control of traffic in the metropolitan area from a joint local authority to a government-appointed representative ad hoc authority. Indeed, traffic was placed under the exclusive control of the Commissioner of Police by the Brisbane Traffic Act of 1905. Similarly, a statutory board consisting of government nominees was entrusted with the construction of a new Victoria Bridge after the former structure was destroyed by the floods of 1893,[7] though it was placed under the control of a joint metropolitan local authority soon after it was constructed.[8]

Before the depression of the early 1890s, the local authorities were dependent upon the government for a large proportion of their revenue and all of their loan funds. Ever since Brisbane and Ipswich were incorporated as municipalities in 1859 under the NSW Municipalities Act of 1858, government endowments had been a critical item of revenue for local authorities. Initially endowments operated on a sliding scale beginning as a pound for pound subsidy on the general rates raised for the first five years and cutting out completely after fifteen years. But under the Municipal Endowments Act of 1876 they were granted a pound for pound subsidy on general rates raised and later also granted on the same basis on general health rates. Divisional boards were granted a double endowment for the first five years after incorporation. The period was increased to ten years by the Divisional Boards Endowment Act of 1885.

Not surprisingly, the amount of endowment paid to local authorities increased rapidly as the economy developed and their activities expanded. Indeed by the 1885-86 financial year the amount paid in endowments to local authorities had risen to £198,783 4s 1d. Since the government anticipated that the payments would continue to increase by between £40,000 and £50,000 a year, it concluded that the treasury must be protected against this heavy drain on its resources. The 1887 local government and divisional boards legislation therefore limited global endowment payments to £85,000 and £165,000 for municipalities and divisional boards, respectively, to be paid to local authorities in proportion to the amount of rates raised. The change in policy was attributed 'to the rapid increase in the amount of endowment payable; to the difficulty of estimating the amount which should be placed each year on the estimates for this purpose; to objection to the power of local authorities, by varying their rates, to force the community at large to endow them; to the inefficiency and inequality of a system whereby central Government raised money for local works; and to the desire to compel local authorities to be both more economical and more efficient'.[9]

The government took the opportunity to make definite arrangements for the continuation of the endowment of local authorities when the endowment provisions of the local government and divisional boards legislation expired in 1890. The onset of the depression had already reduced colonial revenues so that the current level of endowment could only be maintained by raising taxes, which the government was unwilling to do under existing economic conditions. Consequently it decided that the amount of endowment would be determined by an annual parliamentary appropriation which would be distributed in proportion to the rates raised by each local authority. Given its acceptance of the principle that local authorities should themselves raise the money they spend, it is not surprising that the amount set aside for endowment payments each year should decrease rapidly from £195,000 in 1890 to £30,000 for the year 1902-03, or that it should be discontinued altogether the following year, despite the recommendations of the Royal Commission that endowments should be increased.

To compensate for the loss of such a critical item of revenue the rating power of municipalities was doubled to 2 pence in the pound of valuation and of divisional boards by 50 percent to 1½ pence in the pound of valuation by the Valuation and Rating Act of 1890 which also changed the basis for local government valuation of land from the annual value to the unimproved value. Although the Royal Commission did not recommend an increase in rating levels, the rate ceiling was raised again to 3 pence in the pound in 1901. In the absence of endowment payments the government felt obliged to double the rating powers of local authorities to 6 pence in the pound in 1910 and to fix the maximum rate at one shilling in the pound in 1920 after inflation had made existing levels unrealistic.

The steep reductions in the endowment payments and their eventual discontinuance were a savage blow to local authority revenues. The depression had induced steep falls in property valuations and, consequently, a disastrous decline in rate revenues. For example, the valuations of property in the Municipality of Brisbane (city after 1902) fell steeply from £8,800,351 in 1891 to £5,744,201 in 1898 and did not recover to £8,735,573 until 1923. Alderman Leslie Corrie reported in 1903 that the £57,000 raised in rates in 1890 was £2500 more than was raised in 1902-03 and that rate revenue in 1902 exceeded the £50,000 raised in 1891 under the new system of valuation by only £4500.[10] Valuations for the whole metropolitan area show similar trends and had the same disastrous effects on rate income. The consequences for local works and services were obviously quite marked.

Between 1890 and 1903 endowment payments to metropolitan local authorities declined steeply from £132,477 1s 10d in 1890 to £18,905 18s 5d in 1894. They stabilised at just over £20,000 for the rest of the 1890s before rising to £37,378 17s in 1900 and then declining to £7005 7s 1d in 1903, the last year of payment. Commenting in 1903 that endowment payments were fast reaching 'vanishing point', Corrie reported:

> In the year 1887, for instance, the amount of endowment received by the Council exceeded £41,000 being only some £1700 less than the total sum raised in 1902 under the increased rate of 1¾d in the pound. In other words, the Council, fifteen years ago, was receiving seven times as much endowment as it received last year.[11]

The withdrawal of the endowment payments was all the more galling to the council because of the extent of valuable property owned by government, churches and charitable organisations which were exempt from local government rating. It was argued that, since government departments expected payment for services rendered, 'the Corporation, for services rendered, should look for a contribution towards rates from Government properties the same as paid by other folk'.[12] The government's only response to the dire financial straits of local authorities was to double the rate ceiling to 6 pence in the pound in 1910. It was even claimed that the withdrawal of the endowment was a breach of contract, especially as the government had introduced a land tax. Alderman Henry Diddams of the City of

Brisbane asserted that not only had there been a breach of faith, but that the government had broken an agreement not to introduce a land tax if the endowment was withdrawn.[13]

Until the 1890s, local authorities were totally dependent on the government for loan funds. Under the Local Works Loans Act of 1880 and its amendments local authorities could only borrow from the colonial treasury. The legislation also fixed the term of loans to accord with the time the work involved would benefit the community, and required annual payments which would not only meet the interest payments but would also liquidate the loan by the end of its term. The onset of the depression forced the government to abandon this policy especially in the case of the municipalities of Brisbane and South Brisbane. Its own financial predicament prevented it from continuing its normal policy of making loans to local authorities. But the depression had also freed up the money market and reduced interest rates. Consequently, the Brisbane Municipal Council was in a position, through the sale of debentures at attractive interest rates, to liquidate all its indebtedness to the government and its bank. Since a municipal loan of this kind would reduce the government's own indebtedness, it persuaded parliament to pass the Brisbane Municipal Loan Act of 1893 which authorised the Brisbane Municipal Council to borrow £225,000 on the open market. The same privilege was extended to the South Brisbane Municipal Council in 1897 and to local authorities in general by the Local Authorities Act of 1902 without removing their ability to borrow from the treasury. The loans were secured on the revenues of the local authorities and permission to borrow had first to be secured from the government. However, treasury officials proved loath to authorise debenture loans so that only a few of the larger local authorities borrowed on the money market before 1919. It was not until the enactment of the Local Bodies' Loans Guarantee Act of 1923 that the government was empowered to guarantee as well as to authorise local government loans raised on the open market.

3.1 Bogged down in wood blocking Queen Street, between Creek & Eagle streets, 1897/98 (JOL)

The change in government policy was of particular importance to the Brisbane Municipal Council since the act of 1893 reduced its interest bill by £3245 per annum. Furthermore the policy change enabled the council to borrow £80,000 under a second loan act in 1896 to implement the most extensive and innovative street improvement project undertaken in the city until 1913, that is, the wood-blocking of George Street between Roma Street and Queen Street, Queen Street, and Wickham Street between Ann and Brunswick streets and the tar-metalling of the intersecting streets for a distance of five chains. An additional £80,000 was borrowed by the sale of debentures in 1900 to liquidate an overdraft incurred because of an over-run in the cost of the wood-blocking project and to finance a range of other city improvements. The wood-blocking project was opportune for it provided an appropriate processional way for the federation celebrations of 1901. The council did not borrow again on the open market until a £170,000 loan to finance city improvements was approved in 1913.

Special legislation also authorised the South Brisbane Municipal Council to borrow funds through the issue of debentures. The South Brisbane Municipal Loan Act of 1897 enabled the council to borrow £105,000 to pay off its indebtedness to the government and its bank, while the South

Brisbane Loan Act of 1901 authorised the council to borrow £100,000 at the rate of £20,000 a year to carry out drainage throughout the municipality as required by the Commissioner of Health. The borrowing powers of the council for the same purposes were increased by £50,000 in 1906 and again in 1912. However in 1921, while the government authorised the council to sell debentures to retire the 1897 loan of £105,000, it also required the council in future to borrow all loan funds under the provisions of the local authorities act.[14]

3.2 After wood blocking Queen Street, its posts festooned with gum branches for Christmas, c.1902 (JOL)

The Greater Brisbane Scheme was first conceived during the 1890s as a consequence of the fragmentation of metropolitan local government during the 1880s, due to the excessive use of the right of communities to petition for incorporation as new local authorities and the government's readiness to accede to such requests. The petty local authorities created by this process were ill-fitted to perform the vital functions entrusted to them and their number made cooperation more important and yet more difficult to achieve. As early as 1891 the Booroodabin Divisional Board sought unsuccessfully to amalgamate with the Brisbane municipality and not surprisingly the Royal Commission canvassed the idea of a greater Brisbane as a means of providing a comprehensive administrative system for the city and reducing the overhead costs of metropolitan local government. At the time, the idea of a greater city was under consideration in both Sydney and Melbourne. When evidence was being taken there were suggestions of an enlarged city with a ten-mile radius and of the possibility of special legislation to bring it into being. With a government which favoured the amalgamation of local government areas and an expectation that amalgamation would result in an enlarged city authority, it is not surprising that the commission should recommend that an early enquiry should be held into the fusion of certain local areas.[15]

Although the suggestion was not taken up immediately, Alderman J. Nicol Robinson, mayor of Brisbane, inspired by a similar initiative in Sydney, called a conference of metropolitan local authorities in 1900 to discuss the creation of a greater Brisbane. He informed the conference that the new authority should have a unitary structure and control an area with a five-mile radius. Since the delegates did not have the authority to commit their councils or boards to such a scheme, the discussions were merely exploratory. A second conference appointed a five-man committee to draw up a greater Brisbane scheme for consideration at a later meeting. The report of the committee clearly favoured the introduction of a greater city because of the advantages it would bring – greater efficiency and economy in administration, uniformity of approach to city-wide undertakings and a better system of representation. It recommended that the municipalities of Brisbane and South Brisbane, the Division of Booroodabin and parts of the shires of Ithaca and Toowong should be amalgamated into a greater Brisbane, with provision for additional areas to be included from time to time. But already interest in such a scheme had begun to wane since only delegates from Brisbane, South Brisbane and Toowong attended the third conference in February 1901. When the conference was again convened the attendance was so poor that the project was abandoned.[16]

Although Robinson's initiative had failed, the concept of a greater Brisbane persisted. The Municipality of Brisbane and the Division of Booroodabin agreed to amalgamate during 1901 and the City of Brisbane Enlargement Act of 1902, which consummated the union, made provision for the annexation of other suburban authority areas. Indeed, the amalgamation was hailed as the first step in the achievement of a greater Brisbane.[17] However, suburban local authorities were not anxious to join Brisbane in a 'greater' city as the response of the South Brisbane council to an advocate of union with Brisbane indicates: '... it is not at present the intention of the Council to amalgamate with the Corporation of the City of Brisbane'.[18] Public interest in the scheme was kept alive by the *Brisbane Courier*, enthusiastic citizens and supporters in the Brisbane City Council, government and parliament.[19] The concept had become so popular that it became a plank in the policies of both the Liberal and Labor parties during the 1915 Queensland parliamentary elections.[20]

Having won the election, the Labor party concluded that Greater Brisbane would have to be imposed on the local authorities if it was ever to become a reality and opted for a greater city with a ten-mile radius rather than the five-mile radius advocated by the local authorities. Having presented exploratory greater Brisbane bills in 1917 and again in 1923, it secured the passage of the City of Brisbane Act in 1924 which created a city with a ten-mile radius, wide functions and extensive powers.

The federation decade was a critical stage in the development of local government in Queensland and Brisbane. The Royal Commission on Local Government of 1896 undertook a comprehensive and painstaking review of local government in Queensland in general and in Brisbane in particular. Its recommendations formed the basis of the development of local government law and practice in Queensland for more than three decades. The system of local authorities established in the Brisbane metropolitan area was essentially unchanged until the introduction of Greater Brisbane in 1925. The onset of the depression in the early 1890s prompted the government gradually to reduce and then discontinue the endowment of local authorities, thereby forcing them to adjust their budgets to the revenues they could raise from rates and other local sources. It also concluded that it was no longer in a position to provide all the loan funds required by local authorities, initially authorising the municipalities of Brisbane and South Brisbane to borrow on the open market and then in 1902 extending the privilege in law to all local authorities. The concept of a greater Brisbane also took root during the federation decade, but it was another two decades before it became a reality.

Entrepreneurs & Engineers

04

'Intelligent Progress' or 'Injurious Curse'?

Manufacturing and the business of federation

David Cameron

By the end of the nineteenth century the colony of Queensland had worked to position itself in the British Empire and world commodity markets, principally in the export of wool, minerals, meat, dairy foods and sugar. Queensland's economic status at this time was still that of a developing peripheral economy linked to the fluctuating market demands of Britain and Europe. Queensland governments recognised this and were heavily involved in promoting rural economic development aimed at exploiting opportunities for trade with Europe. After federation the Queensland government attempted to balance the post-colonial economy by encouraging rural intensification (closer settlement agriculture) and the expansion of the domestic market. A rural development mantra gripped the state's political leaders for several decades while the development of Queensland's manufacturing industries was virtually ignored. Despite serious threats from increased competition of cheaper interstate imports following federation, Queensland's manufacturing sector consolidated itself and continued to develop those industries where it had a natural competitive advantage. Despite many negative economic ramifications associated with the introduction of federation in January 1901, the most significant negative factor affecting Queensland's economy during the first decade of the twentieth century was the long drought of 1898-1903. Federation and the long drought combined to create very difficult trading conditions for Queensland's manufacturers, the drought being more instrumental in retarding the sector's development than post-federation free trade between the states.

The Queensland economy at the time of federation

While the Queensland economy should be referred to as a single entity, it must be stressed that it was not an homogeneous economy. Rather, it was, and still is, a heterogeneous entity comprised of several distinct regional economies subject to wide variations in climate, resources, geomorphology, markets and population densities. These regions were all at different stages in their economic evolution, and relied upon common as well as specialised markets. The broad generalisations made here are qualified by a recognition that circumstances varied between regions and that the focus of this study is the impact of federation on manufacturing in Queensland and, in particular, Brisbane.

The divergent economic experiences in Queensland's south, centre and north can be better understood when examined in light of economic-geographic factors and location theory. Queensland's decentralised economy, dependence on primary production and patterns of trade can be understood to reflect various aspects of Urban Base, Centre-Periphery and Agricultural Location theories.[1] In Queensland's historical development the links between economic forces, geography and demographic patterns are fundamental. Queensland's economic geography has been shaped by the interplay between fluctuations in external demand for rural commodities, (principally wool, meat, minerals and later, dairy products), based upon urban expansion in Europe (as distinct from domestic urban demand), and the spatial diversity of its resources, types and access to transportation, and the systemic linkages of the importation of human and financial capital with the principal export markets.[2]

This understanding takes into account the spatial and aspatial aspects of Queensland's trade cycle, stressing spatial features as the dominant factor that simultaneously induced decentralised production and urban growth and restricted centralisation, urbanisation and more intensive agriculture. In Queensland the dominance of the metropolis was not as pronounced as it was in the southern capitals. Queensland's decentralised economic structure evolved in response to external patterns of trade and capital investment which stimulated dispersed rural commodity production across Queensland in productively and economically suitable locations. A series of vital export-import nodes located along the coast serviced their respective hinterlands, providing direct access to foreign markets generally bypassing Brisbane. This economic and demographic structure had a fundamental impact on the popular, business and political attitudes to federation and the social, economic and political impact of federation in Queensland.

At the turn of the century Queensland's economy was in a semi-depressed state as a result of a prolonged drought which began in 1898 and continued until 1903. Between 1890 and the Great Depression of the early 1930s, Queensland's gross domestic product increased by almost 150 percent. In broad terms, for Queensland's economy this involved a recovery by 1895 from the early 1890s depression, with slow growth or stagnation until 1903, the result of a tight money market and decreased production because of drought. Economic growth resumed during the mid-1900s, despite two periods of recession (1901-04 and 1908). However, this positive trend once again stalled with the out-break of war in August 1914.[3] Official estimates for the total value of production of all Queensland's industry sectors are not available until after 1910. Nevertheless it has been calculated from the available data that the gross value of production for all of Queensland would have been approximately £17 million in 1901. This had increased to £26.4 million by 1911 and to £36.8 million by 1913.[4] This represents an overall increase in value of something in the order of 116 percent between 1901 and 1913.

Despite the economic ramifications associated with the introduction of federation in January 1901, the most significant individual factor affecting Queensland's economy during the first decade of the twentieth century was the long drought of 1898-1903.[5] That is, federation and the long drought combined to create very difficult trading conditions. Indeed, Queensland's trade statistics demonstrate that the negative economic effect of the long drought, combined with trade difficulties associated with federation, lingered until at least 1904. Evidence of the impact of the drought can be seen in the figures for Queensland's total trade (imports and exports), which declined sharply between 1899 and 1901, and generally stagnated until 1904. Clearly an economic slump was evident prior to the proclamation of federation on 1 January 1901. In general terms, trade grew steadily across the board from 1905 (with the exception of a minor slump in 1908) to 1914. Exports slumped and imports increased as a result of reduced rural production between 1901 and 1903. It is evident that a major structural shift occurred in the ratio of interstate to foreign imports arriving in Queensland during this period. In effect, in many cases the foreign imports were simply replaced by interstate imports rather than eroding Queensland's domestic production. During the period 1900 to 1910, imports into Queensland from interstate grew from about 20 percent of all imports to more than 50 percent. But despite this Queensland's manufacturing sector managed to increase its workforce from 26,000 to 34,000 (+ 31 percent) and value of production from £79.2 million to £127.2 million (+ 60 percent) over the same period.

The trade figures prior to 1910 include interstate imports and exports. They demonstrate how significant Australian domestic trade was to Queensland's economy. Queensland was exporting more than it was importing from interstate in 1910. Total trade was valued at £16.8 million in 1900 and £25 million by 1909. With the exclusion of interstate trade, the total was reduced to £13.6 million in 1910 and stood at £19 million by 1913.[6] Despite a slump in exports between 1901 and 1903, Queensland achieved a positive balance of trade with a surplus of exports over imports throughout the entire period 1900-1913. In 1900 exports accounted for 57.1 percent of the total value of Queensland trade, by 1913 this had increased to 64.8 percent.[7]

Pastoral industry

Any examination of Queensland's historiography and official statistics clearly demonstrates the importance of the pastoral sector to the development of Queensland's economy. The long drought had a dramatic and negative impact on the state of the pastoral sector, with many pastoralists in dire straits by 1902. After the drought, the pastoral sector recovered well, and despite some isolated regional slumps, which occurred between 1903 and 1908, the years from 1908 to 1912 showed good returns. Indeed, by this time confidence within the industry was at its highest since the 1880s.[8] Pastoralists and pastoral companies increased investment across the industry (sheep and cattle) with growth experienced in both the number and total acreage of pastoral properties.[9]

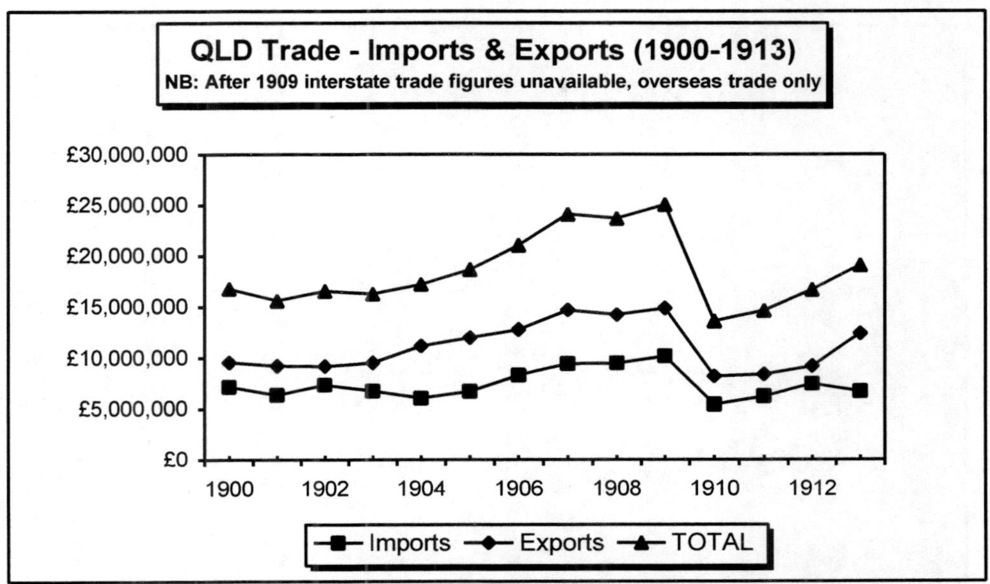

The post-drought confidence was based on a combination of good seasons and high prices which manifested itself in high levels of capital investment directed towards corporate consolidation, infrastructure improvements, breeding programs, upgrading and expansion of existing meat processing works, and the establishment of new meat works.[10] In the political-economic sphere pastoral interests continued to maintain their privileged position. However, change was in the wind, organised labour became increasingly influential in the political sphere and the concept of developing irrigation schemes became the new catch-cry of the advocates of closer settlement agriculture.

Agricultural industry

Prior to the 1890s the economic contribution of the agricultural sector to Queensland's economic development was limited and commercial cropping has been described as economically 'insignificant' at this time.[11] Generally it can be shown that the agricultural sector had failed to expand significantly prior to 1900, despite repeated attempts by Queensland governments to promote closer settlement agriculture. Queensland continued to import vast quantities of agricultural produce well into the first decade of the twentieth century.[12] At this time the total area under intensive agriculture in Queensland comprised less than 5 percent of Australia's productive agricultural land. Agricultural land in Queensland by per capita area was 0.9 percent compared to a national average of 2.4 percent.[13] Of the 297 million acres of land occupied or alienated in Queensland by 1900, a mere 457,397 acres were under crop![14]

Nevertheless there was a general expansion in the agricultural sector from around the time of federation to 1910. This rural intensification was fuelled by 'the impetus of an unlimited and continuous optimism about the possibilities of land settlement'.[15] The period between federation and World War I saw the process of rural development accelerate on the back of high confidence, high prices and high expectations. The most significant impetus to the growth of agriculture was the increase in domestic demand for its produce. Here the pattern of development did not generally involve a process of agricultural intensification promoting the growth of service centre/market towns and cities. Rather, the reverse was generally the case. All of Queensland's coastal cities preceded their hinterlands and commercial agricultural production. The coastal ports relied on pastoral exports and not, primarily, domestic markets. Once the domestic market grew to a point of critical mass the development of a viable agricultural sector became possible.[16]

4.1 Threshing at Wallumbilla, 1899 (AHC)

The irony in this is that the populist yeomanry ideal, which reviled urbanisation, in fact actually relied on the growth of urban populations to underwrite the economic viability of closer settlement agriculture. In this, Australia was somewhat unique. Essentially, without a high degree of urbanisation, expansion of the agricultural sector was not possible. The economic importance of urban concentrations lies in their dual role as point of assembly and distribution of primary produce and their internal economic dynamic of demand and consumption. Urban concentrations develop a functional economic momentum, or in other words, their own consumer demand oriented production.[17] Therefore, the rise of global markets, European and North American urbanisation and rapid urbanisation in Australia in the late nineteenth century, created the demand for the type of agricultural products Queensland was well situated to produce.

Mining industry

The greater part of Queensland's historiography on the mining sector involves histories of individual mines, mining towns, and regional fields, with a strong emphasis on mining activity in north Queensland.[18] This, of course, reflects the relative importance of the north's mineral resources to the development of mining in Queensland. The distribution and diversity of minerals mined in Queensland is impressive with metals such as gold, copper, silver, tin, iron and zinc, and vast coal measures in central and southern Queensland. Mining has played a significant role in driving the economic and demographic development of many areas in Queensland, especially the north. The mining sector was also especially important in providing a market for Queensland manufacturers, particularly in metals processing and engineering.

Federation and the Queensland economy

The development of several distinct regional economies within Queensland, each with their respective urban hubs, has generated a high degree of regional economic independence and encouraged attitudes of self-reliance and self-determination. Regional parochialism associated with this economic evolution would prompted a great deal of political friction when the debate over federating the colonies arose during the late 1880s. Apart from Samuel Griffith's key role in the federation debate of the early 1890s, and despite the often raucous debate at times carried on in Queensland, the colony generally played only a marginal role during the crucial years of the federation campaign in the latter part of the decade.[19] Queenslanders had, it seems, more pressing issues on their minds, including drought and economic depression.

The height of the federation debate coincided with the peak of the drought-induced depression in Queensland. The combination of drought, economic downturn and uncertainty over whether a trade war with the southern states would result after the removal of protective colonial tariffs, created a sense of economic and social insecurity across many areas in Queensland. The sense of foreboding expressed by sections of the business community, and by many of their employees, stimulated renewed activity by separationists who again agitated for the creation of new states or colonies in central, northern and far north Queensland. The separationists, quite rightly, recognised that federation would effectively extinguish any future political hope for the establishment of new states within Queensland.[20]

Attitudes towards federation in Queensland cannot be referred to in any homogenous sense. There were distinct differences of opinion associated with various contributing factors such as class, occupation, political orientation and geographic location.[21] The Queensland government also took its time in putting the question of federation to the people.[22] Eventually 65% of registered Queensland voters turned out for the referendum in September 1899, a good response considering the national average was 61%. Of these, only 55% voted in favour of federation. In all, a mere 36% of the total registered voter pool in Queensland actually voted in favour of federation, so the victory for the affirmative was less than comprehensive. Indeed, the 55% 'yes' vote was the lowest affirmative vote recorded in any of the colonies.[23]

Alan Jenkins argues that those people advocating federation were united by a mixture of patriotism, nationalism and a sense of homogeneity of origins shared by the colonies. The victory, however, was a hollow one as there remained a solid core of support for an independent colony of Queensland. Large sections of the labour movement in Queensland were especially hostile towards federation, and calls were made for Queensland to cede from the commonwealth and form its own independent nation.[24] As early as 1902, Thomas Plunket, MLA for Albert, moved in parliament that Queensland secede in protest over the perceived negative impact federation had on Queensland's industries. Plunket's motion was wholeheartedly supported by the Townsville Chamber of Commerce, which should come as no surprise as Townsville and neighbouring Thuringowa were staunch centres of separationist activism and support.[25]

As well as the loftier issues of national loyalty, nationalism and continental defence, Jenkins identifies economic issues as being the primary motivation for the way various sections of Queensland society voted in the federation referendum. Moreover, economic circumstances influenced peoples' subsequent perceptions of how federation impacted on Queensland's economy. Simple correlations between specific industry groups, for example, are difficult to demonstrate because sections within various industries differed in their position depending on their location and principal markets.[26]

As the views of the Maryborough Chamber of Commerce reveal, regional and intra-industry variances in attitudes towards federation were of paramount importance and were almost always economically motivated. Furthermore, these views were based upon how various industries in a particular district were performing at the time and how they were expected to fare after federation.

Jenkins suggests that, as a 'rule of thumb', the districts where industries were more prosperous were inclined to support federation, while those who were less prosperous voted against the perceived threat federation posed to their livelihoods. Indeed, in north Queensland the 'yes' vote was particularly strong and Jenkins argues that this was in a large part due to the general prosperity experienced in the north during the 1890s.[27]

Not everyone in the north was supportive. Anti-federation pro-separatist sentiment was particularly strong around Townsville prior to federation.[28] and afterwards, as expressed, for example, by the support shown by the Townsville Chamber of Commerce for Plunket's secessionist motion put to the Queensland parliament in 1902. The more closely one examines the economic dividend or deficit that an industry group or representative perceived would result from federation, the more convincing Jenkins' 'prosperity' thesis becomes.[29]

The vote on federation can generally be divided into two broad demographic categories. The 'no' vote was dominant in an area 'of about 100 square miles in the extreme south-east and a smaller section around Rockhampton. The rest of Queensland showed varying degrees of loyalty towards federation, with support being strongest in the extreme north and west'. The votes cast in favour of federation in south-east Queensland, and Brisbane in particular, contributed to the overall success of the pro-federation campaign in Queensland, and ultimately for the rest of Australia.[30]

Business and federation in Brisbane

The economic goal of the Commonwealth Constitution was to create free trade between the states and to introduce a tariff on various imports which together would bolster Australia's overall economic performance and potential for growth. The Courier editorialist in January 1900 supported a revenue-based tariff but whole-heartedly opposed any form of protective tariff.[31] The Courier's position was one not shared by Brisbane's manufacturers.[32] They supported a universal protective tariff but were ill at ease over what impact free trade between the states would have on the viability of their factories. From the perspective of the colonial governments, the insertion of the Braddon clause into the constitution was a fiscally painful compromise.[33] This would inevitably reduce state revenue bases in favour of increased centralised commonwealth control over customs and excise revenue and the advent of a universal tariff.[34] The membership of the Brisbane Chamber of Commerce was divided over the issue, depending on members' perceptions of how federation and tariffs would affect their businesses.[35]

Outside of Brisbane the attitudes towards federation of the other employer groups across Queensland varied considerably. The Townsville and Rockhampton Chambers of Commerce opposed federation. The MCC and the Queensland Employers' Federation were generally supportive of the change.[36] Some considered the economic implications of federation for Queensland as a double-edged sword. On the one hand, it offered an expanded national market for Queensland's primary produce, especially its sugar and beef. On the other, the same tariff-free status favoured the full competitive advantage of the southern manufacturers over the apparently weaker Queensland manufacturing sector. Some manufacturers either objected to or supported federation depending upon the nature, size and financial strength of their particular manufacturing business and the perceived benefits, or otherwise, and the effect that free trade between the states would have on their particular industry, market share and costs of raw materials.[37]

The Brisbane Chamber of Manufacturers

The advent of a Queensland-based chamber of manufacturers is generally accepted as having occurred with the formation of the Queensland Chamber of Manufacturers in 1911. However, it is evident that a Brisbane-based chamber, called the Brisbane Chamber of Manufacturers, was established much earlier in October 1899.[38] The BCM was formed at the instigation of A.J. Carter, president of the Brisbane Chamber of Commerce. Carter had convened a special meeting in response to the concerns of BCCom members that Queensland's manufacturers should be represented at the Intercolonial Tariff Conference of Manufacturers in Melbourne in November 1899. The conference of manufacturing representatives from across Australia was called to debate and draft a united position on the tariff regime to be adopted after federation.[39] The BCCom executive was adamant that it would not be involved in the conference, presumably because of some dissent among its ranks between free-trade and protectionist members.[40] Nevertheless, as economic historian Alan Lougheed asserts the BCCom supported vigorously the efforts of the Queensland Chamber of Manufacturers to be represented at discussions on the federal tariff.[41] This view is supported by the fact that Carter, a pro-federalist and prime mover behind the formation of the BCM, was at the time the president of the BCCom, and a firm supporter of assistance to encourage the development of secondary industries in Queensland.[42]

Carter called a meeting of interested manufacturers, which was held in Brisbane on Friday 27 October 1899. At this meeting it was intended to propose names of prospective delegates to attend the Intercolonial Tariff Conference in November and to enlist support for a formal meeting to establish a permanent body to be called the Brisbane Chamber of Manufacturers and also to select delegates for the Melbourne conference. The meeting to establish the BCM was held in the BCCom's meeting room in the Courier Building on Monday 30 October 1899. Thirty manufacturing firms were represented at the meeting, and J. Stodart MLA and J.F. Howes attended as representatives of the Bundaberg and District Sugar Manufacturers Union.[43] Carter stressed that the conference organisers would not tolerate any delay, and the appointment of Queensland delegates would have to be made immediately. Carter proposed that an organisation should be established that was 'absolutely independent' of the BCCom. Carter refused a nomination that he chair the meeting, probably so as not to create a conflict of interest with his position as president of the BCCom. On the motion of R.W. Thurlow, D. Campbell MLA was appointed as chairman of the meeting. J.C. Donaldson then formally moved that a Chamber of Manufacturers be formed, and this was seconded by J.H. Forrest. The motion was put to the vote and carried unanimously.[44]

A provisional committee was then elected.[45] A ballot was held and Gibson, Hart, Morrow, Donaldson, Hayes, Stewart, and S. Larard were elected as delegates to the Melbourne conference. Larard was also appointed secretary to the BCM as well as to the Melbourne delegation.[46] Another meeting was held on the following day, 31 October 1899, when manufacturers John Crase and John Reid were added to the committee. Forrest was appointed as honorary treasurer and Campbell appointed chairman. The chamber placed notices in newspapers across Queensland seeking suggestions from interested parties about the tariff issue, which the delegates might subsequently address at the conference.[47] In the context of the federation debate the BCM soon emerged as a popular body with Queensland's manufacturers. Indeed, Carter's efforts were soon vindicated; within three months, membership of the BCM had grown to represent more than 100 employers.[48]

Three intercolonial conferences of Chambers of Manufacturers were held in Melbourne (1899), Adelaide (1900) and Sydney (1900).[49] The *Brisbane courier* gave tacit support to the BCM delegation, despite reservations about what long-term impact protection would have on the economic progress of Queensland. The editorial conceded that a protective tariff was 'well-nigh a certainty' and that a tariff designed to stimulate infant industries was acceptable.[50] In the *Courier*'s opinion the BCM delegations which attended the Melbourne and Adelaide conferences comprised moderate protectionists, who were not likely to accept any extreme measures that would damage Queensland or the nation as a whole.[51] It is clear from C.R. Hall's research on the history of the Chamber of Manufacturers of NSW, and contemporary press reports, that the Queensland delegations were primarily concerned with the impact that a commonwealth tariff would have on the competitive position of manufacturers after the withdrawal of colonial tariffs, and the viability of the sugar industry based upon white labour. This was flagged by the attendance of Stodart and Howes of the B&DSMU at the first meeting of the BCM. Angus Gibson, after outlining the position of the Queensland sugar industry, successfully proposed that the conference endorse a preferential tariff of £4 per ton to be applied to Australian-grown sugar. This in effect meant that the Australian public would have to subsidise the higher wages paid for white labour in the Queensland sugar industry.[52] Following the Melbourne conference, the BCM established thirteen sectional committees to assess the tariff's potential to either assist or hinder the separate branches of the manufacturing sector and to draft recommendations for the BCM delegates to take to the second conference held in Adelaide in May 1900.[53]

From the limited records available.[54] it appears that the BCM, and its later incarnation, the QCM, were principally involved in lobbying with other employer organisations for changes to, or the limitation of, industrial legislation, particularly in respect of wages boards, awards, workers' compensation, and commonwealth and state conciliation and arbitration.[55] The other dominant issue was tariff protection, where lobbying in support of it was, at times, undertaken in concert with the relevant trade unions. The BCM was active in directly lobbying the government, through correspondence and deputations, and was sufficiently organised to host the first national conference of the Federal Council of Chambers of Manufacturers in August 1904. The government supported this endeavour, allowing the conference to be conducted on board the Queensland government's steamer *Lucinda*.[56] The conference forwarded resolutions to the Queensland government urging it to stand firm against moves to increase commonwealth powers through commonwealth conciliation and arbitration legislation, and to maintain its commitment to the existing Wages Board procedures, with unpaid representatives of both parties with a Supreme Court judge as final arbiter.[57]

A press report of the annual general meeting of the BCM held in June 1904 notes that the chamber had forty-nine members, having increased membership by seven firms during that year.[58] There were several prominent businessmen on its executive and council, including John Reid (president 1903-05), H.J. Diddams (printer and publisher) and J.K. Stewart (vice-president 1903-05), R.W. Thurlow (president of the BCCom and member of the QEF), J.J. Verney (later a representative of the Central Queensland Employers Association), E.C. Barton, A. Forsyth, George Hiron and T. Morrow (both biscuit and confectionery manufacturers), and Emil Sachs (tinsmith).[59]

The chamber was obviously very active as it met fifteen times during the year to discuss matters such as the adulteration of foodstuffs, Workers Compensation Bill, Federal Patents Bill, Commonwealth Industrial Arbitration and Conciliation Bill, and to support the preferential tariff for Empire trade. The group also endeavoured to organise an industrial exhibition for Brisbane to showcase the diverse range of local manufactures. The executive felt the work of the chamber since federation had been most valuable as much 'objectionable' legislation had been withdrawn or suitably amended as a result of their intervention.[60] Despite all this activity, however, the BCM appears to have gone into abeyance after 1905, with contemporary reports making no mention of the Chamber's activities after November 1904.[61] The demise of the Chamber was most probably the result of the tariff issue being settled by 1902, and therefore, the initial impetus for its establishment was lost. Indeed, many of its members were actively involved in other more established organisations, such as the BCCom, the QEF and in many other metropolitan and regional trade or industry-specific employer groups, and probably felt that their interests were better served by these organisations.[62] This also suggests that the economic impact from interstate trade associated with federation was not sufficiently onerous to prompt the BCM to complain loudly about it.

The Brisbane Chamber of Commerce

For many, the answer to the question of federation was not a simple 'yes' or 'no'. The pros and cons of federation were often difficult to assess; the issues were not printed in black and white - more shades of grey. The attitudes of some of the executive members of the Brisbane Chamber of Commerce reflected the guarded optimism of many members. They were not entirely convinced of the real economic benefits that might be derived from federation. Nevertheless, they felt such a union of the colonies was inevitable and in the long-term interests of Queensland.[63]

In 1899 A.J. Carter, president of the BCCom, expressed his support for federation. He argued that federation would benefit all the colonial economies thanks to the establishment of a single national free market. Federation, he stressed, was needed to displace parochial attitudes with a more 'broad-minded view' which would allow Australia to make 'intelligent progress'. Carter's view was both that of a pragmatist and an economic nationalist. He could see the national sense behind federating but also knew that the Queensland government was heavily reliant upon its customs revenues and it was therefore important that Queensland had a strong hand in drafting the new constitution in order to protect its interests.[64]

Nevertheless by 1903 some members began to argue that federation was beginning to have a direct identifiable and negative impact on Queensland's economy. Abraham Hertzberg, president of the BCCom in 1903, was scathing in his attacks on the negative influence he perceived federation had wrought on Queensland's economy. Hertzberg's bitter criticism of federation comes as no surprise; along with another BCCom president, A.J. Thurlow, he was a prominent member of the anti-federation Anti-Convention Bill League.[65] In Hertzberg's opinion, federation had been economically 'most injurious' to Queensland because it created more legislative restrictions and regulations on trade, encouraged the further concentration of trade and industry in the southern cities, and promoted the dumping of cheap goods on the newly interstate tariff-free Queensland market. Hertzberg claimed that federation had reduced the volume of trade handled by Queensland merchants by over £2 million. He contended also that lower real wages had cut consumer-spending power and undermined the stability of the Queensland economy. Furthermore, he predicted that federation would be a curse on Queensland's future prosperity and would seriously retard its economic development.[66] This, Hertzberg asserted, could be seen in the decline in business investment in Queensland, a particular problem for the manufacturing sector where he claimed many had suffered 'to the point of extinction'.[67]

Hertzberg also blamed federation for the demise of the Philp government, claiming that the premier's strong support for it had amounted to political suicide.[68] In 1905 he continued his attack on federation in a lengthy and detailed letter published in the *Brisbane courier*. Here Hertzberg quoted copious statistics and he estimated that the negative economic impact of federation was 'two and a-half times as bad as were the effects of the worst drought [1898-1902] ever experienced in Queensland'.[69]

While federation adversely affected the viability of, and employment in some areas of the manufacturing sector, its negative impact was exacerbated and distorted by the lingering effects of the long drought. This situation was conceded by R.W. Thurlow, BCCom president in 1908, who admitted that the early years of federation had been difficult, but with the return of good seasons, the states had recovered well. Thurlow's reconsideration of federation was rebutted by Hertzberg the following year. He again argued that Queensland's under-development was due to federation and the situation could have been much different had they 'not, in a weak moment, given away our birthright'.[70]

Hertzberg's views are somewhat extreme and exaggerate the negative impact of federation upon the viability of Queensland's manufacturing sector. A detailed historical analysis of the contemporary statistical evidence demonstrates federation as the lesser culprit when compared with the long drought and pre-existing structural inadequacies.[71]

Queensland manufacturing and federation

That the Brisbane Chamber of Manufacturers appears not to have railed against the perceived negative impacts associated with federation is understandable as ultimately the qualitative and quantitative evidence suggests that, overall, federation generally had a positive rather than a negative impact on Queensland's economy and industries. The negative aspects ascribed to federation by contemporary observers and later by historians and others have been somewhat overstated.[72] If federation had impacted as severely as has been claimed, then a clear pattern of greatly increased interstate imports and decreased domestic production in Queensland would be evident. In fact the official statistics demonstrate only mild growth in imports in the years immediately after the implementation of federation until 1906 (after which interstate imports increased rapidly) and stronger overall growth in exports, accompanied by a strong expansion in production.[73]

Although a complete breakdown of imports by type is not available for the period prior to 1910, those that are available do not indicate any significant increases that can be solely attributed to a flood of interstate imports into Queensland immediately after colonial tariffs were removed.[74] Essentially, the growth trend in overall trade which emerged out of the 1890s depression was interrupted prior to federation because of the long drought, but re-emerged from 1903. That is, trade in Queensland revived when the drought was broken - rain resuscitated the state's industries. The economic contractions experienced during the early to mid-1900s, while in part a response to interstate free trade, were most significantly influenced by the depression associated with the long drought and regular fluctuations in cyclical demand and production. The drought overshadowed the economic impact of federation, not only in Queensland but across many areas of Australia.

Great care must be taken when considering the impact that the introduction of a 'free' market between the states after federation and the drought had on trading conditions in Queensland's manufacturing sector in the early 1900s. To adequately assess whether or not federation had an adverse impact on Queensland's manufacturing sector a close examination of the statistical record is required. When considering the statistical profile of the manufacturing sector prior to the First World War, a number of anomalies and inconsistencies must first be addressed. The two major sources of statistical data for Queensland's secondary industries are the Queensland Government's 'Factories and Shops Reports' and the *Statistics of the Colony/State of Queensland (Statistics)*. One of the most intriguing anomalies arises from the inconsistencies between the data collected and published in the Statistics and those recorded in the F&SR. It appears that data were collected for the *Statistics* by the Registrar-General's Department, while the F&SR were compiled by officers assisting the Chief Inspector of Factories & Shops, first within the Home Secretary's Department (1896-1902), then the Public Works Department (1903-07), and later the Department of Labour (1908-30). The data series recorded in the *Statistics* were, however, drawn from a variety of sources, including data supplied by the Chief Inspector of Factories and Shops from 1896, and collected from a number of administrative

4.2 Stanley Coach Works, Stanley Street, South Brisbane, c.1902 (JOL)

districts, the boundaries of which were altered over the years. The Registrar-General's Department generally classified its factory districts in accordance with police district boundaries.

The F&SR series, on the other hand, used similar, but sometimes less or more inclusive boundaries, as stipulated under the provisions of the various Factories and Shops acts 1896-1920. The expansion of existing district boundaries and the inclusion of new districts, from six to fourteen between 1900 and 1921, meant that more factories eventually came under the provisions of the Factories & Shops acts. Factory classifications were also changed over time. Before 1896 an enterprise was classified as a 'factory' if materials, raw or manufactured, were worked into another shape or form with the aid of machinery, and employed two or more employees. With the passage of the Factories & Shops Act 1896, the classification was altered to four or more employees, using machinery powered other than by hand. In 1901 the classification reverted to two or more employees, which remained in force until the end of 1907. In 1908 the classification was changed permanently to four or more hands. This chopping and changing in classification makes linear comparisons very difficult. For example, the change of factory definition to two or more hands in 1901 led to the inclusion of a host of smaller factories, especially in the areas of tailoring, dressmaking and other industries where females were employed, and also bootmaking and blacksmith workshops. The number of factories recorded in the F&SR after 1908 provides an alternative range of statistics which suggests that there were many more factories operating in Queensland than is revealed in the *Statistics*. Another anomaly arises because the F&SR series reveals only those factories registered in the various districts as declared under the Factories and Shops Acts. Large areas were therefore not included in its census. It has been estimated that the factories not counted in the official census would have amounted to approximately 10 percent of the official figure, a not insignificant discrepancy. This estimate was made by Colin Clark, the Queensland State Statistician in the late 1930s.[75]

When considering the number of factories operating at the turn of the century, data from the *Statistics of the State of Queensland (Statistics)*, published annually in the *Queensland parliamentary papers*, appear to clearly indicate a significant decrease in the number of factories in the years immediately following federation. In 1899 the number of factories employing four or more hands increased from 1795 in 1898 to 2610 by 1899, dropped to 2078 in 1900, and then increased slightly to 2110 in 1901 under the new two or more hands classification.

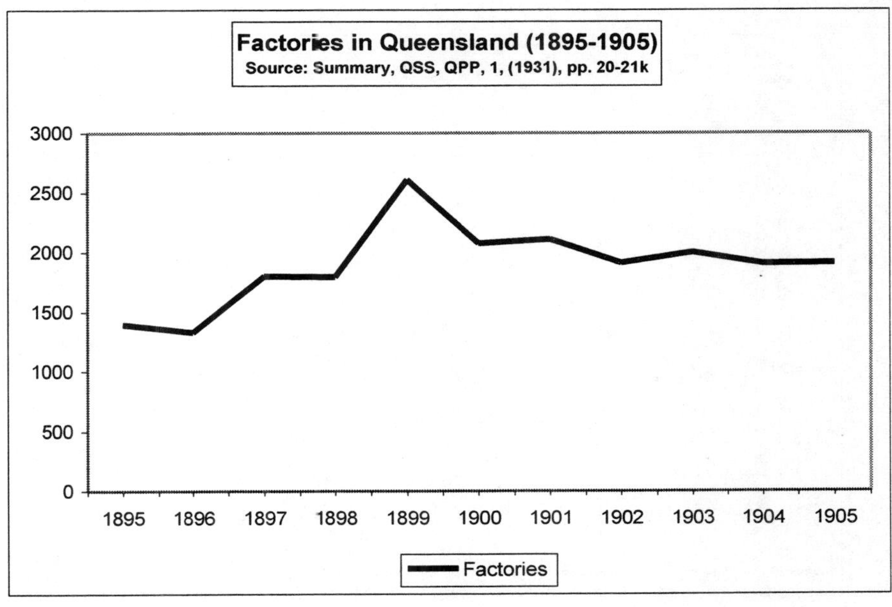

These figures illustrate two important points. First, a rapid and dramatic decline in the number of factories occurred in the year *prior* to federation. Second, the decline continued despite the apparent slight increase in overall factory numbers in 1901 because this figure takes in a much larger pool of factories with the change in classification from four to two or more employees. If factory numbers had remained stable between 1900 and 1901, then the difference in the figures for those years would have been much greater as the number of factories employing between two and three hands was significant. The number of factories declined further to 1890 in 1902, corresponding with the worst year of the long drought (1898-1903). The decline in factory numbers was initially accompanied by an appreciable reduction in manufacturing employment between the years 1901 and 1903. This fall was followed, however, by strong employment growth from 1904 to 1908 and even more robust expansion from 1910 through to the First World War.[76]

The post-federation trading conditions and the long drought affected manufacturing enterprises in a number of ways depending upon the location of the business, its size, access to capital, number of employees, type of products manufactured, location and size of markets, and degree of interstate or foreign competition. For example, it appears that federation and the drought had a rather negative impact on many smaller factories. This trend is not clearly identifiable in Queensland's statistical records. However, commonwealth statistics do provide a brief statistical snapshot indicating that a decline occurred in the number of small factories in Queensland following federation.[77]

Between 1900 and the outbreak of the First World War manufacturing employment increased by 63 percent. Recorded employment in Queensland's factories grew from 25,953 in 1900 to peak at 26,172 in 1901, then decreased to a low of 19,286 in 1903 near the end of the long drought. After the drought broke, manufacturing employment again grew rapidly to more than 30,000 by 1910 and had exceeded 42,000 by 1913. Another important statistical indicator is the value of productive output. The value of *output* represents the wholesale price of manufactured goods produced whereas the value of *production* indicates the value added by the manufacturing process to the value of the raw materials consumed. That is, the value of production equals the value of output less the cost of materials consumed in the process of production. The trend in the value of manufacturing is similar to that seen in manufacturing employment. Output increased from £7.9 million to almost £9 million between 1900 and 1901, slumped to £7 million between 1902 and 1903, then recovered rapidly to £23.7 million by 1913.[78]

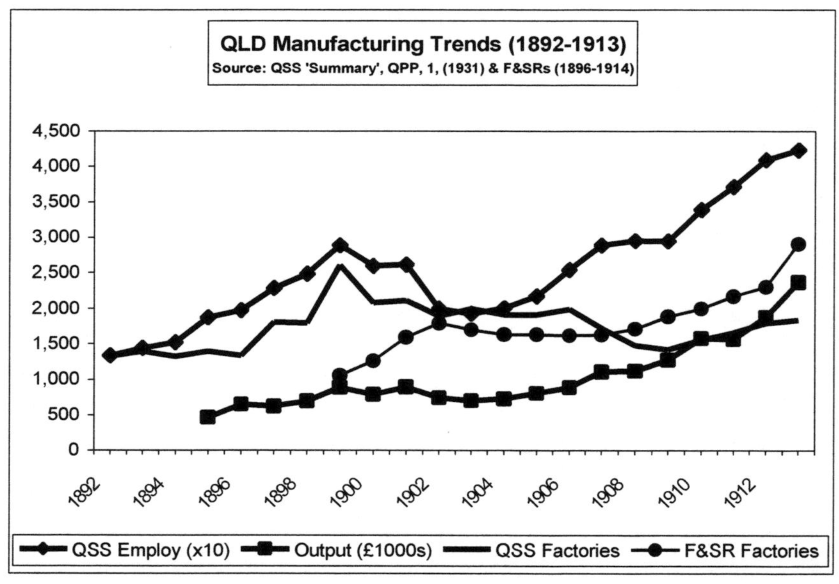

While the trend is indicative of a decline in the number of manufacturing establishments during this period (1900-08), the change in statistical classification of factories distorts and exaggerates this decline. There was, nevertheless, a real reduction in the overall number of factories and it is fair to argue that some of this decline can be attributed to the change in trading conditions after federation. It is reasonably clear that some elements of the manufacturing sector were directly and adversely affected by increased competition from southern manufacturers as a result of federation, particularly smaller operations such as bootmaking, jam-making, bedding and upholstery making, and also some lines of clothing manufacture. However, E.J.T. Barton, a respected writer and commercial agent at the time of federation, did not stress an abundance of economic impediments associated with federation. Barton's assessment of the progress of Queensland's manufacturing sector, principally Brisbane's factories, published in a contemporary promotional publication on Queensland's economic and social development in 1909,[79] supports the argument that the impact of federation on the viability of Queensland's manufacturing industries was rather more marginal than has been generally perceived.

Barton notes some initial negative impacts associated with federation in the biscuit and confectionery baking, jam and fruit preserving, boot and shoe-making, and tanning industries, because of an influx of cheaper imports from interstate. Far from decrying the evils of federation, however, Barton argues, for example, that after an initial influx, interstate imports of biscuits tended to make inroads into the Queensland market generally at the expense of foreign imports and not the local product. In another instance, Queensland jam makers responded to stiff import competition by shifting production to Queensland fruits, such as pineapples, mangoes and bananas, thereby

4.3 Granlunds Tannery workers, Free St, Newmarket, 1899 (JOL)

developing a specialist competitive advantage and winning new local and interstate markets. The tanneries, on the other hand, actually had plenty of orders but had trouble meeting them as they found it very difficult to secure the raw materials they needed, because most Queensland hides were being exported interstate where they fetched higher prices. In the boot and shoe-making trade, despite the relatively higher wages paid in Queensland, the threat from cheaper imported boots and shoes waned as consumers maintained a preference for locally produced footwear. Barton also notes that other industries, such as saddlery, harnessware, leather trades, clothing, engineering and wood-working, actually benefited directly from increased trade after federation.[80] For example, increased imports of cheap New Zealand timber was offset by growth in the export interstate of timber manufactures from Queensland, such as doors and window frames.[81]

In Barton's view, any disadvantages appear to have been more than counter-balanced by new opportunities and increased trade.[82] This view was also shared by several regional chambers of commerce who did not blame federation for the economic downturn. The MCC, for example, was dominated by manufacturers and a great many Maryborough businesses relied upon them. As a body, the MCC were committed protectionists and fully supported federation.[83]

This view supports Jenkins' argument that, generally speaking, the stronger industries tended to profit from the competition and as a result increased their market share.[84] In essence, large enterprises grew even larger, swallowing up their local competition, and in some cases, began exporting goods interstate.[85] For the manufacturers who were severely weakened by the economic impact of the drought, the simultaneous onset of free trade proved too much, and many of the more marginal operations were adversely affected by interstate competition.[86]

Moreover, like the other eastern states, Queensland faced the economic changes of federation with the added burden of a drought-induced depression - a burden experienced more acutely in Queensland due to its greater economic reliance on pastoral production and the relative severity of the drought. The troubles that beset the manufacturing sector in the early 1900s can, to a larger degree, be attributed to the combination of a drought-induced depression, existing structural deficiencies (older, less efficient plants, high wages), restricted access to development capital, virtually no government assistance, and the impact of post-federation competition.

It has been shown here that the decline in factory numbers began to occur *prior* to federation. Moreover, recovery in terms of employment and production commenced from 1904 after the bad years of 1901-03 which corresponded with the depth of the drought-induced depression. Indeed, the recovery from the drought was the key issue in the fate of the manufacturing sector during this period. When all the relevant statistical factors are examined in combination, including the number of factories, employment, and the value of output and production, it is evident that the perceived negative impact that federation had on the manufacturing sector is not as severe as has been suggested.[87] Some historians, however, have acknowledged both the disadvantages and advantages that federation had on the manufacturing sector and have found on balance that its overall impact was either marginal or benefited Queensland manufacturing.[88] As some of the more reflective contemporary observers have conceded, the sharp economic downturn that occurred between 1901 and 1903 was mostly the result of reductions in production and trade associated with the long drought, the negative impacts of which have for too long been unfairly foisted upon federation.[89]

05 Brisbane engineers at federation
The men and their institutions

Bill Oliver

Before considering the role of Brisbane engineers at the time of federation, it is important to understand the term engineering and the vast range of tasks which fall under this umbrella. Put simply, engineering is the application of *ingenuity* to the analysis and solution of problems, often social problems such as safety, public health, mobility and so on. It is not a domain reserved solely for professional engineers, as will become clear.

The institutions of engineers

In Britain the distinction between military and civil engineers was formalised in 1818 with the establishment of what was to become the highly esteemed Institution of Civil Engineers, based in London. Suddenly, engineering became professional! [1]

Twenty-nine years later in 1847, the Institution of Mechanical Engineers was established. This reflected the beginning of specialisation in the profession. It was not until 1888 that the Institution of Electrical Engineers was formed from the then existing Society of Telegraph Engineers. A curious consequence of this aspect is a book published in 1852 all about the *electric* telegraph. Its author was one Edward Highton, CE, an associate (not a full member) of the Institution of Civil Engineers.[2] He apparently saw himself as more civil than mechanical. At that stage, he presumably had nowhere else to go. The close link between mechanical engineering and electrical engineering had not then been established.

Queensland's first engineers were, of course, military engineers, members presumably of the Royal Engineers, accompanying the first convict settlement. Until 1890 almost all engineers in Australia were British trained, so that for all practical purposes, Australian engineering was an extension of British engineering.[3] Much the same situation applied ten years later at federation.

In 1890 the Queensland Institute of Mechanical Engineers was formed with about forty members. From about the third meeting, all meetings were held in what press reports of the meetings referred to as the Institute Room in the Courier Building. After approximately fifty meetings, the QIME seems to have gone into recess in 1895 under the general pressures of the early to mid-1890s. Until then, proceedings of the meetings were reported, often in considerable detail, in one or more of the *Brisbane courier, the Queenslander* and/or *the Building and engineering journal.*

In 1898 about 3 years after the demise of the QIME, there emerged the Queensland Electrical Association. In the 18 years of its existence, the QEA published a continuing series of papers presented to its meetings, of which parts or all of at least thirty-three survive.

In 1900 on the eve of federation, and perhaps out of touch with the times, the Queensland Institute of Engineers was formed. It was intended to be a reviver for the defunct QIME and to provide for civil engineers who did not have a local institute of their own. In 1911 it seems to have absorbed the QEA. As with its predecessor, the QIME, it presented series of interesting papers, invited visitors to attend and take part in discussions, and sought association with like bodies such as the Institute of Architects in relation to learned society activities, including their mutual interest in promoting technical education.

It was not until after the First World War that inter-colonial isolation among Australian engineers was formally ended by the foundation in 1919 of the Institution of Engineers, Australia. Engineers apparently needed 18 years to get their federation act together. The more British of the engineers refused to join the colonial outfits, preferring to retain membership of one (or more) of the Old Country's societies, notably the Institution of Civil Engineers, of Mechanical Engineers, or of Electrical Engineers. Each had its various grades of membership: Member, Associate Member, Associate, Student.

This paper will examine some of Brisbane's 'federation' engineers, their achievements, their foibles and the learned societies into which they formed themselves or to which they belonged, and some aspects of their employment environments.

The early engineers

The Queensland Division Heritage Panel of the Institution of Engineers, Australia, has published, within two small volumes, fifteen years apart, potted biographies of eminent Queensland engineers, 34 in volume 1 and 51 in volume 2. Of these, some 20 were practising in or around Brisbane at federation.[4] They were all men of the age of steam and animal horsepower for transport. They, with other engineers perhaps less eminent, engineered provision for the Brisbane of the day with drainage, water supply, coal, gas, coke, candles, electricity, sugar, flour, soap, ice, telegraphs, telephones, bricks, timber, buildings, factories, foundries, municipal and emergency services, railways, trains, tramways, trams, bridges, roads, carts, carriages, wharves, cranes, docks, slipways, navigable waterways, lighthouses, ferries and ships.

At federation, the Brisbane men - there were no women 'professional' engineers - did *not* engineer aeroplanes, airports, air conditioning, automobiles, microwaves, radios, stainless steel or televisions. They were fiddling with a municipal hydraulic power system and sewerage.

The engineering environment 1900-01

Brisbane's population at the turn of the century was about 122,000.[5] The colony and its capital city were only beginning to emerge from the dual disasters of major recession and flood. Recovery had progressed considerably by 1896, but there were still major problems. By federation the colony was two years into the grip of its longest ever drought, one that was to be far worse than that of 1885-86, lasting until 1903. Pugh's almanac in its review of 1900, reported on the gravity of the situation:

> ... the terrible condition of our western country from drought, scores of pastoralists being absolutely ruined or on the brink of it; and of course all business there is at a standstill. ... So certain is the slow recovery from this situation that the Premier intimated that Public Servants' salaries may have to be reduced.

A question in the Queensland Legislative Assembly deploring the reduction in the frequency of trains travelling between Rockhampton and Brisbane drew the reply from the Secretary of Railways that all the rail services were being examined with a similar intent.[6] Flow in the Brisbane River upstream of Mount Crosby slowed to subterranean flow between waterholes.[7] and the Brisbane Board of Waterworks made several formal requests to the Brisbane Municipal Council to reduce its street-watering program. There was a major build-up of water hyacinth in the virtually still waters of the Bremer and Brisbane rivers, and their tributary creeks still carrying water. The drought affected the whole of the east of the continent, and had a depressive effect on the fortunes of several engineers.

Alfred Brady, Edward Cullen and Henry Stanley

Three engineers practising in Brisbane at federation were awarded the prestigious 'Telford Premium' by their learned society, the Institution of Civil Engineers, London. All three attained the highest grade of membership and the right to the post-nominal MInstCE - Member, Institution of Civil Engineers. Only one of the three seems to have had any involvement with the local learned societies, and that was short-lived.

Alfred Barton Brady, MInstCE (1856-1932) was Under-Secretary and Government Architect and Bridge Engineer in the Department of Public Works. Brady's major monument in Brisbane was the Victoria Bridge built to replace the 1874 bridge destroyed by the first of the February 1893 floods.

5.1 Victoria Bridge decorated for the Duke and Duchess of York and Cornwall's visit, May 1901 (JOL)

Completed in 1897, it was of similar design to his Burnett Bridge in Bundaberg, begun in 1890 and completed in 1900. Brady was a member of the ICE, London, and submitted a paper on the Victoria Bridge to that Institution in 1902, for which he was awarded its Crampton Prize. Along with somewhat less robust structures, it was decorated as part of the federation celebrations. It was replaced by the present Victoria Bridge in August 1969, after which it was dismantled. Part of the ornamented southern abutment designed by architect J.S. Murdoch was preserved and is regarded in a recent publication as a heritage site.

Earlier in 1900, Brady was awarded the prestigious Telford Premium by the ICE for a paper on the 1896 Lamington Bridge at Maryborough, which replaced another 1893 flood casualty. Queensland

5.2 C.J. Oldham, BCC Engineer for Subdivisions, viewing the dismantling of the 70-year-old Victoria Bridge from the downstream walkway of its 1969 successor (AHC)

Division of the Institution of Engineers, Australia, thanks to the thoughtfulness of a Brisbane firm of architects, recently acquired the Brady Telford Premium trophy, a beautifully illustrated book of British structural work of the nineteenth century. The book has been rebound, and is held in custody at Engineering House in Upper Edward Street.

As Government Architect and Engineer for Bridges from 1892 until his retirement in 1922, Brady's signature appeared on drawings for all major public buildings, many if not most (or even all) of which may have been the work of architects under his control. The only building for which

5.3 Central Railway Station, early 1900s. Note the barrel roof designed by Alfred Brady (AHC)

Queensland architects of the 19th century awards him any credit is Central Railway Station, completed in July 1901, and then only for the roof, since replaced in 1966.[8] Before upgrading to engineering, Brady had behind him eight years of architecture (1872-79), and could well have had substantial input into the design of the many public buildings whose designs bear his signature. He claimed that he always advised on 'arrangement, style and materials'. Detailed design was apparently left to others, supervised presumably by his senior assistant, the architect Thomas Pye.

The new Central Station, due for completion by federation, was sufficiently complete for it to be used in May for the royal visit of the Duke and Duchess of York and Cornwall for their journey south after the Brisbane celebrations of the previous days.

Although a royal commission investigated the Public Works Department in 1900 and Brady was criticised, he emerged as Under-Secretary of the Department as well as Government Architect and Bridge Engineer, offices he retained until his retirement at the age of 66 in 1922.[9]

Edward Alexander Ernest Cullen, MInstCE (1861-1950) The floods of 1893 virtually obliterated the dredged channels in the Brisbane River. They had been more or less restored by mid-1895 to pre-flood depths and widths. In 1899 work on the Lytton bar provided a depth of 20ft (6.1m) for a width of 300ft (90m), the length of the cutting being 920ft (280m). This formed part of a scheme prepared in 1897 by Cullen,[10] the Brisbane-born engineer who was to become Chief Engineer, Marine Department, in 1900, and Engineer for Harbours & Rivers in the re-formed Department of Harbours

& Rivers in 1902.[11] The period 1893-1902 was one of ongoing reorganisation of the maritime departments.

Upstream of the Victoria Bridge, as far as the Bremer junction, a much smaller provision was made for the Ipswich river traffic, a minimum depth, at high water of 6-7ft (1.8-2.1m). As a port, Ipswich was effectively dead in the water.

Despite the satisfactory Brisbane channel depths, siltation beside the wharves was a problem in 1900, and ships were getting ever bigger. A major problem was that many of Brisbane's wharves were 'sufferance' wharves, owned by shipping companies and tolerated under sufferance. The berths needed dredging, and the onus and cost of dredging lay with the wharf owners. If the owner failed to provide due depth, trade was handicapped and the port discredited. This was just one of the problems that Cullen had to live with at federation. Others included job insecurity attaching to relentless reorganisation, the financial slump due to the drought and the poor performance of the expensive new suction dredge *Samson*, the larger and more expensive of two designed and sold to the government by one Lindon J. Bates of the United States. Bates apparently negotiated through the Portmaster, Captain Almond, in order to sell his expertise and dredge designs to the Queensland Government. The *Hercules*, also a Bates' design, but of half the power of *Samson*, performed quite satisfactorily. However, after an initially good start on 26 April 1900,[12] reported on in glowing terms by Almond, Samson's performance deteriorated alarmingly, so much so that questions were asked in parliament. By this time, Portmaster Almond had authorised payment to Bates and retired.

The problem of water hyacinth in the Bremer and Brisbane rivers and their tributaries was raised in the Legislative Assembly. In response to questions about the subject, the treasurer blithely replied on 10 December 1900 that the Marine Department had been instructed to take immediate steps to eradicate the pest.[13] One might well wonder how many immediate steps Cullen would have needed to take to deal with that particular problem.

Cullen was also involved with Brisbane drainage construction programs carried out first by William Nisbet in Brisbane after the floods of 1875, and again in 1896. Cullen's name appears on drawings of drainage in George, Roma, Turbot, Ann, Herschel and Adelaide streets, dated 1877, and on one for Sneyd Street dated 1896.[14]

After presenting a paper on 9 August 1901 to the fifth monthly meeting of the QIE about dredge pumps.[15] he was not apparently further involved in the activities of that institute. Later in his career, he was to join the Telford Premium club for a paper presented to his Institution of Civil Engineers on the improvement of the Port of Brisbane.[16]

Monuments to Cullen are the Kangaroo Point and New Farm quarries and possibly some remnant sections of the revetment walls constructed along the lower reaches of the Brisbane River during his terms of office, using stone from those quarries.

Henry Charles Stanley, MInstCE (1840-1921) Railways accounted for 70 percent of government expenditure between 1880 and 1900. Stanley, brother of architect Francis D.G. Stanley, was Chief Engineer for the latter half of the period. A dozen railway bills were passed in 1900, requiring £500,000, and providing much-needed employment.

Stanley was a railway bridge designer of considerable note, his most rewarding design being the elegant Albert Bridge at Indooroopilly over the Brisbane River, completed in 1895 to replace another casualty of the 1893 floods. For a paper on this, presented in 1898, his Institution of Civil Engineers, London, awarded him the Telford Premium.[17] This monument to Stanley is still in service, albeit visually spoilt by graffiti on the decorative sandstone abutments and by being sandwiched between two of three other bridges since constructed between Indooroopilly and Chelmer.

Things then seemed to fall apart for Stanley. A new station being built at Wooloowin involved a roadway overbridge which was erected in the wrong position. On 29 August 1900 in answer to a question, the Secretary of Railways informed parliament that responsibility for the blunder lay with the Chief Engineer.[18] On 14 November 1900 after Stanley's retirement in September, the house was informed that the cost of rectification was estimated at £16,150.[19] The new Central Station was not completed until July 1901, nearly six months after an already extended completion date, and not in time for the May royal visit.

Stanley's nadir was probably reached when on 25 July 1901 a question was asked in parliament suggesting that his forthcoming retirement at age 61 amounted to a push. This came after thirty-five years continuous service to the state railways since 1866.

Joseph Badger, Ned Barton and John Hesketh: The electricals

The generation of electricity by steam-driven dynamo produced for the last two decades of the nineteenth century an experience for the wider society just as explosive as the one that occurred in the decades after the personal computer arrived on the scene in 1981.[20] Brisbane, its suburbs and Ipswich were into the early throes of the most convoluted industry developments they were ever to experience, further complicated by the tactics of the main power industry of the age, the gas industry, directed against the entry of the new electric competition.

Electric arc lighting was first demonstrated as a novelty as early as 1878. A generator was later set up in 1881-82 in the premises of J.W. Sutton in Foundry Lane, at the north side of what is now Post Office Square, for a demonstration of street lighting.[21] By 1892 electricity had been generated at six sites throughout the town, at such places as Roma Street railway yards, at Edison Lane, by Barton & White to serve the GPO, the Brisbane Newspaper Company and the old Printery from where underground cables were run to enable electric lighting of parts of Parliament House.[22]

By federation, two very substantial power stations had been built right in town. One was constructed in 1896 for Barton's Brisbane Electric Supply Company at Ann Street where the Brisbane Administration Centre now stands. It was here that the first steam turbine in Brisbane was installed in 1901.[23] The other power station was erected in 1896-97 at Countess Street for the Brisbane Electric Tramway Company. The Tramway Company also had two smaller generators at its Logan Road, Woolloongabba, and Light Street, Fortitude Valley, depots.[24]

5.4 Countess Street Power House, 1920s (JOL)

In terms of involvement with, support and enthusiasm for, local engineering societies, E.G.C. (Ned) Barton, Joseph Badger and John Hesketh were the antitheses of the seemingly reluctant Telford Premium trio. Barton and Hesketh were successively employed in 1886 and 1896 as the Government Electrician. During Hesketh's term in office, the title changed to Government Electrical Engineer. Barton resigned in 1888 to go into private practice, but was retained in a part-time capacity until Hesketh's appointment in 1896.

5.5 Interior of Countess Street Power Station, c.1912, built under the supervision of Joseph Badger (JOL)

Ned Barton, MIEE, FRGS, AMIEAust. (1858-1942) Barton, pioneer-in-chief of the Queensland electricity industry, was trained in England and Germany. He threw himself vigorously into the formation in 1890, and then the affairs, of the QIME and its 1900 successor the QIE. He was also active in the formation in 1898 of the QEA, of which he was, as he was later to be of the QIE, the second president. In addition to his involvement with the local societies, Barton was local honorary secretary to the Institution of Electrical Engineers IEE, of which he may have been the first Australian-born member. Being fluent in French, German and Italian, he went to England in 1915 to serve in the Department of Munitions and later the Department of Naval Information.[25]

In the opening of his April 1901 inaugural address to the QIE entitled 'Theory and practice', Barton issued a warning about federation, probably revealing himself as a reactionary isolationist:

> ... the new century has brought us federation [f] and will therefore bring us into an atmosphere of keen competition, wherein the Engineers [E] will have to supply the means for the commercial community to survive ... Were it not for our new dredges, Sydney would be the only harbour on our seaboard fit to survive. Were it not for our steamers, railways, and telegraphs and telephones, the very vastness of this State [S] would render its wealth inaccessible.[26]

The reference to dredges was probably made in acknowledgement of the attendance at the meeting of Edward Cullen, then Chief Engineer of the Marine Board. It seems that Cullen was the only member of the ICE, Telford Premium club, ever to attend a meeting of a Queensland engineering institute.

Barton was a tireless teacher. He presented several papers to the QIME, the QEA and the QIE, and seems never to have lost an opportunity to promote technical education. He was president of the Council of the Brisbane Technical College in 1905, and was on the first senate of the University of Queensland when it was formed in 1910. He was active on the Brisbane scene for at least thirty years.

The disciplines of mechanical engineering and electrical engineering are now closely linked. However, it is safe to say that Barton was the first in Queensland, and possibly in Australia, to personify, demonstrate and document that link of the two disciplines for the benefit of the engineering societies of his time. The variety, extent and quality of his input to the affairs of the societies have seldom if ever been matched.

Electricity supply and communications

After nearly forty years of telegraph service, the new phenomenon of the telephone was taking hold. The first line to Ipswich was established in 1896, the trunk line extended to Toowoomba before federation. In the last (1900) annual report of the Queensland Posts & Telegraphs Department, it was recorded that there had been a 20 percent rise in subscribers to 1100, and that 3,500,000 calls had been made during the year ended 30 April 1900, 2,250,000 of them from Brisbane.

John Hesketh, (1868-1917) was Barton's successor as Government Electrician, a title by which he was addressed by the Ipswich Municipal Council in 1896,[27] the year of his appointment.[28] The council sought his advice in September of that year on street lighting of Ipswich with 5000 lamps. In the short term, the council used his report, specification and cost estimates to approach the Ipswich Gas Company, well entrenched as provider of the town's street lighting, for a reduction in its gas prices. As in Brisbane, it was not until 1917 that electricity got its toehold into street lighting.

Early in 1897 the Brisbane Municipal Council sought Hesketh's advice, and in July of that year, he advised the council that it should undertake the generation and distribution of electricity as a proper and remunerative task.[29] At about the same time, he provided the Ipswich Municipal Council with a list of the financial results of electricity undertakings in the UK, none of them to be sneezed at.[30] He presumably plied the BMC with the same information. By federation, Hesketh found himself deeply involved in the ducking and weaving that was to characterise the supply of electricity in Brisbane for the next eight decades.

Hesketh was elected inaugural president of the QEA, presenting his first paper on the role of the association in promoting electrical engineering education. During the eight years of his membership, he presented four papers, including the only paper on electricity generation.

His predecessor in telegraphy, W.J. Cracknell was gazetted captain in the Queensland Torpedo and Signalling Corps in 1878 during the 'Russian Scare'.[31] Hesketh carried on the tradition, being gazetted captain in the Brisbane Company of Submarine Miners. John Baillie Henderson was included in the same list, as lieutenant.[32] This could have been either the analyst or his namesake the Engineer for Water Supply.

Hesketh left Queensland for Melbourne in 1906 to become Chief Electrical Inspector of the Commonwealth Department of Posts & Telegraphs, which took up the reins from the states in March of federation year. He died aged only 49 in 1917. An obituary described him as a striking personality, possessing initiative, industry, ability and courage.[33] Perhaps he acquired or strengthened these qualities as a result of eight years as meat in the triple-decker electricity sandwich between the BCC, his friend Ned Barton and the gas companies.

Transport

Cabs were all horse-drawn, and in response to an enquiry in 1899, the BMC informed Marchant & Co. on 10 July that use of the public streets by motor cars would require enabling legislation before permission could be given. A Mr Thurlow helpfully provided the council meeting of 14 May 1900 with a copy of the London laws regarding use of road locomotives.

Cross-river ferries, controlled by the local authorities, included four vehicular 'horse' ferries, operating from Bulimba, Charlotte Street, Moggill and Indooroopilly. Two smaller steam-powered ferries carried passengers only. Porridge-powered rowing boats, 20 ft (6m) long, capacity 16 passengers, were operating at seven locations from Toowong to Bulimba.[34]

The tramway system had been electrified in 1896-97. As the city and suburbs grew, the tramways also spread out, increasingly in competition, to the apparent consternation of certain parliamentarians, with the suburban system of the state railways. It was asked in the Legislative Assembly in September 1901 if it was the intention of the government, in granting a loan of £4000 to the Toowong Shire Council for formation of a new tram track, to assist the Brisbane Electric Tramway Company to compete with the state railway.[35] A fall-off in patronage of suburban trains at Albion, Wooloowin and Clayfield was brought to the notice of the Legislative Assembly later that month after the new tramline to Clayfield was opened and operated with twelve trams running along it.[36]

Joseph Badger, (1851-1934). Badger, a flamboyant American, was the moving force behind the Brisbane Tramway Company Limited, registered in London, with its office and main power station on state railways' land at Countess Street. The Brisbane Tramway Construction Company ordered major electrical equipment from General Electric, which sent Badger to Brisbane to install it. He arrived in May 1896. After completion of the electrification, he was appointed Manager of the Brisbane Tramway Company Ltd, and stayed on for the next twenty-seven years, becoming General Manager and later Managing Director. He personally drove the first tram from Logan Road to the Victoria Bridge.[37] The Toowong route, constructed later, terminated near Badger's residence 'Belle Vue', in Miskin Street, and for a time carried Badger's private tram, onto which he would invite influential friends such as Sir Augustus Gregory, and probably the Shire Clerk and Engineer of Toowong, William E. Irving. When the BMC proposed a riverside drive and promenade through the Domain from the southern end of Alice Street to Edward Street, Badger was quick to offer a tramline along the drive, and to light the Botanic Gardens. Typically for Badger, these offers were not committed to paper.

With the spread of tramlines into the suburbs, there were twenty-four miles of route, serviced by more than sixty tramcars, came electric power supplies to private premises adjacent to the tramlines. Suburbs which benefited included East Brisbane, Ithaca, Paddington and Hamilton, and Musgrave Park and Botanical Gardens. The tramway power system also energised the state railways' lighting system and tunnel lighting between Eagle Junction and Indooroopilly.[38] According to the Railways annual report for the year ended 30 June 1901, the light was 'all it was intended to be - namely an assurance to timid passengers; and the cost is one fourth of the previous system of keeping the carriages lit by gas all day'.[39]

In 1900 Badger inaugurated the Tramways Band, which gave concerts at various locations beside tram routes including Dutton Park, Musgrave Park, Botanical Gardens and Hamilton. The band disbanded in 1911.

Known widely as 'Boss Badger', and associated in the minds of many with the 1912 strike resulting from his refusal to allow union members to wear their union badges while on duty, he nevertheless provided Brisbane with an excellent tram service throughout the twenty-seven years of his stay in Brisbane. Shortly before federation, the asset value of the company was already £1,150,718.19s.5d.[40]

Along with Barton and Hesketh, Badger was, in 1898, a founding member of the QEA. Although he competed with Barton in the market for supply of electricity, both men were active in the affairs of the QEA for the full twelve years of its existence. Badger was a frequent seconder of votes of thanks and participated in discussions, but there seems to be no record of his ever presenting a paper. He was president in 1905-06. In the early days of the QEA, he made his Countess Street Tramways Company office available for meetings.

Gas

Two gasworks supplied Brisbane's needs at federation, at Newstead and at West End. The gasworks' engineers seem to have been J.H. Tomlinson of the Brisbane Gas Company Ltd (Newstead) and John Davies of the South Brisbane Gas and Light Company Ltd (West End). Davies was the South Brisbane Company's first engineer, designer of the original works. Tomlinson, from a Birmingham gasworks, arrived in 1880, returning to England for a time in 1886 to deal with manufacturers supplying the equipment for the new works to be built at Newstead.[41] Davies' successor, W.S. Moore, was active in the QIE from 1903 to 1908, but neither Davies nor Tomlinson seems to have been involved with the QIME or the QIE.

Water Supply: Alexander Stewart and Hugh G. Foster Barham

Water supply, controlled by the Board of Waterworks, was pumped from the Brisbane River at Mount Crosby, raw into the mains, without any treatment other than a brief settling in the small high level reservoir at Mount Crosby; or, if one were lucky, gravitated from Enoggera or Gold Creek reservoirs, but also raw and untreated into the mains. From time to time, luck would run out, particularly when Mount Crosby water was pumped into Gold Creek reservoir, causing mass putrefaction and necessitating waste of millions of gallons in order to rid the system of the putrid blend. In Brisbane, federation came twelve years before filtration, and then in 1912, only the Board's precious little Enoggera supply was filtered. Mount Crosby supply, much more in need of treatment, was to wait a further seven years for filtration.

Alexander Stewart, CE (1842-1900) was Chief Engineer of the Brisbane Board of Waterworks before federation. He was in charge for the major works of construction, first of Gold Creek reservoir in 1882-86, and later of the Mount Crosby pumping station in 1889-92. After serving the board as its Chief Engineer for the preceding fourteen years, late in March 1900 Stewart received six months notice that his services would no longer be required. He completed his last engineer's report to the board on 27 April 1900, and died of sclerosis of the liver and other complications a week later on 4 May 1900, aged 59. Illnesses of this type were not uncommon among engineers and others unfortunate enough to have been involved with the construction or operation during its early years of the Gold Creek Dam. The board had become aware that its Chief Engineer had a problem, and the way they saw fit to deal with it was apparently to dismiss him.[42] The board had been widely and justifiably criticised about the quality of water, and used Stewart as a scapegoat, killing him in the process.[43]

The Brisbane River eventually reached such a low flow that in January 1901 Joseph Stewart, the Water Board's resident engineer at Mount Crosby, sent teams of labourers along the riverbed to dig channels between waterholes so that the Mount Crosby pumping station could function on a part-time basis.[44] A temporary weir was built out of sandbags immediately downstream of the pumping station intake. In 1902 a more permanent 10ft (3.0m) high concrete weir was built. Replaced in 1926, its remains are still visible. Stewart's temporary successor as Acting Water Board Engineer was his assistant *John Preston*, who disappeared from the scene early in 1901.

Hugh G. Foster Barham at thirty-four was appointed for a term of three years in January 1901, at the princely salary of £700 per annum. A qualified and experienced engineer, from the old country, he soon made his presence felt. He started work in March 1901. With his fourteen years' experience of work on four British waterworks behind him, Foster Barham quickly identified and articulated several shortcomings in the overall system. However, he was apparently premature in asking for improvements and rapidly fell from favour with most of the members of a board not eager to accept criticism of any sort, let alone from one of its employees. Foster Barham had the temerity to ask for a qualified assistant engineer and, of all things, a motor car. He had inherited as assistant engineer the son of the former Secretary, and later a Board Member, Lewis Adolphus Bernays. Maurice Bernays' qualifications and waterworks' engineering experience were effectively non-existent, he being a fitter by trade.[45] Foster Barham succeeded in sidelining Bernays, was granted a bicycle and, in 1902, a new desk.[46]

At the end of his contract term in 1904, the Board offered Foster Barham continued employment on a monthly notice basis, with salary at the rate of £500 per annum, reduced from £700. Two friends on the board, Mayor Lee and George Phillips, were outraged at the board for having dragged Foster Barham across the world to endure such humiliation. However, two friends were not enough. Foster Barham tried to negotiate £600, but the two Board members who had had the knives out for him from very early in his term won the day and Foster Barham resigned. After a holiday in New Zealand, to where he eventually retired, he served in Korea for several years. Ominously, on the day he resigned, a large slump developed in the Gold Creek embankment.[47] Foster Barham was perhaps fortunate to be departing.

Municipal engineering

Brisbane's sewerage was still at the preliminary design stage, in the hands of the Brisbane Municipal Council. A start had been made during the 1890s on the basic necessity for design, a contour survey of the Municipality. An apparently insuperable problem was that the only logical outfall to the Brisbane River at Newstead lay within the adjacent Division of Booroodabin. In the meantime, the night carts delivered their nightsoil collections to Victoria Park, for burial. Victoria Park was within Booroodabin Division, the board of which took a rather dim view from time to time of the way the site was worked by the BMC's contractor. Soon afterwards, Brisbane's nightsoil was to be carted out to feed the fish in Moreton Bay.

Toowong had erected a sophisticated nightsoil incineration plant of some kind, about which Town Engineer and Surveyor *William Irving* spoke at a QIE meeting in November 1905, shortly before which the plant had been extended to deal with garbage.[48] A similar outfit seems to have existed at South Brisbane, from which the final product was trucked away by rail, in open 'F' railway wagons, to Chinese gardeners in Enoggera, prompting indignation, outrage and, in October 1901, questions in the parliament.[49]

In town, wood block paving of city streets was all the go, but there were expensive problems of surface slipperiness with the new system, for people and horses alike. Additionally, the Tramway Company was far from compliant with the wishes of the BMC as to their contribution to the cost of laying the blocks. Rightly or wrongly, the problems were laid at the feet of the City Engineer, John Rogers. Despite these problems, the program was to continue for several years.

The council was toying with the idea of a hydraulic power system for the city, similar to Sydney's, but despite considerable promotion by wishful suppliers, some enquiries from architects and business houses, and support from the City Engineer, this was never to eventuate.

W.H. Chambers, Tom Kirk, John Rogers, John Kemp and Tom Kirk (again) were the engineers who served under Brisbane's Town Clerk, William H.G. Marshall, from 1872 until 1916.

Some found more favour with their masters than others. *W.H. Chambers*, the first to be titled City Engineer (his predecessors were described, in the still current British manner as surveyors) seems to have been well favoured. None of the competition entries for design of the Eagle Street fountain was accepted. Despite Chambers' 1863 sacking by the colony's first Colonial Architect, Charles Tiffin, for incompetence, the fountain became a task for the City Engineer. He was to be rewarded by his name being carried into posterity by inclusion with those of the Town Clerk and the aldermen of 1879 on a plaque forming part of the decoration of the fountain. His good fortune with the council continued right to the end of his eleven year term. When he departed in February 1886, he was granted a year's leave of absence with dismissal thereafter.[50]

Tom Kirk, CE, Chambers' deputy and successor, departed in 1888, apparently in similar circumstances. Kirk was later to return for another three-year term as City Engineer in 1909. One of Kirk's assistants was a surveyor, *E.H. Gibbon*, who may have acted in the position after Kirk's 1888 departure. Gibbon was to continue in the service and become senior draughtsman and assistant engineer under Kirk's successor.

John Rogers, AMICE. Times were different in 1899-1900. Following an 'exhaustive inquiry' into all departments of the council, beginning with the city engineers, Rogers, Gibbon, draughtsman J.W. Wright and seven other members of the City Engineer's Department received four months notice of dismissal on 2 April 1900. Rogers was given a reference of kinds, 'testimonial as to length of service, etc.'. He in particular seems to have fallen from favour, and Alderman Thomas Proe, who was to be mayor the following year for the royal visit, had the longest and sharpest knife. The inquiry recommended employment of a Foreman of Works at £300 per annum. Alderman Hall, unhappy that the council's 'spending' department was to be headed by a Foreman of Works, moved that 'Foreman of Works at £300' be replaced by 'City Engineer at £500', but the motion was lost. Interestingly, despite the exclusion of engineers, there was a recommendation to appoint an engineer's clerk.

Rogers' assistant, Gibbon, was something of an old hand, aware of how Chambers and Kirk had been treated on their dismissals, and he and Rogers sought similar golden handshakes. Gibbon applied for twelve months leave of absence on the same terms which had obtained with regard to 'other professional gentlemen who have been connected with the Council'. On 28 June 1900 Gibbon and Rogers were granted six months leave of absence with dismissal thereafter. Proe objected to payment of an honorarium to either of them and by compromise moved the substitution of three months for six months. His motion was defeated, so he then asked if two other dismissed servants, a Foreman of Works, Cherry, and Water Inspector, Payne, would also receive honoraria. The minutes provide no answer to the question. However, on 9 July applications for retiring allowances were received from William Cherry, R.C. Payne and P.P. Waters. Proe seems to have won the day, because on 6 August the council reneged on its June decision, advising Rogers, Gibbon, Cherry and Waters that it could not grant their request for retiring allowances.

Gibbon was given some casual piecework on mapping the layout of the city drainage and Rogers likewise got a few crumbs examining and reporting on rickety buildings around the town. A minute on 15 October suggests that he was not paid for these services. On 28 May before the request for a retiring allowance, there was a minute commending Rogers for his work on the celebration of the relief of Mafeking. On 1 October he offered a proposal to furnish a scheme of street decoration for the contemplated visit of the Duke and Duchess of York and Cornwall. He wrote to Ipswich Municipal Council offering his services. He also took legal advice.

Wright was re-employed as draughtsman, possibly along with Payne. An entertainer of kinds, Wright is worthy of particular mention, for at one of the meetings of the QIE, he and an H.T. Phillips, entertained the gathering with song.

At the same council meeting of 6 August 1900, Alderman Proe, of all people, was to second a motion for employment of a City Engineer at a salary of £750 per annum, the vacancy to be advertised in the southern colonies and in the UK. Copies were mailed to the city councils of Sydney and Melbourne, and of Adelaide from which the response quickly came back: if you pay your engineer £750, how much do you pay your Town Clerk?

John Kemp, The upshot of this was a response in June 1901 of fifty applications for the position, the successful applicant being Kemp, an English city surveyor. He took up his post in December 1901 and seemed, at least in the short term, to find favour. In the mayoral minute of 1903 covering the mayoral year 1902-03, Mayor Leslie Corrie paid Kemp a compliment for his foresight in respect of the design of a sewerage system, including as it did the needs of an expanded city. Kemp had also obliged by enclosing an unsightly open drain in Queen Street taking discharge from the Eagle Street fountain. Kemp was appointed Chief Engineer of the Board of Waterworks in 1905, serving with the board until 1912, the last three years reporting to E.J.T. Manchester who was an unsuccessful applicant for the 1905 appointment. Unlike some other UK immigrant engineers of the time, Kemp was an active member of the QIE, and was its president in 1907.

A significant portion of Corrie's 116-page mayoral minute was given over to a litany of serious shortcomings around the city, very well articulated and often in quite florid language. There was no system of building approvals. The total of the surveyed frontages of properties in a city block usually failed to equal the surveyed length of the block, the original 1859 survey plans and field survey marks had either been lost or never forwarded from Sydney after separation. Governor George Gipps had tampered with the first city survey in 1840 and wiped out reserves, squares, esplanades, wide streets, etc. Development control was very much a thing of the future, and developers would, apparently, deliberately plan to stymie development of adjoining properties. There was not a single convenience for the fairer sex to be found in the city. The need for tree planting was covered by a three-line verse.[51]

It is fitting to conclude this survey of federation engineers and the trials and tribulations they faced with some doggerel which Corrie borrowed and adapted from the *Washington star* and thought fit to insert in his mayoral minute at page 26:

The New Pavement

They took a little gravel,
And mixed it up with tar;
They laid it on so level,
'T would suit a motor car.

They dusted it and rolled it,
And when they went away,
K[em]p swore he had a pavement
That would last for many a day.

But F[oste]r-B[arha]m smote it
To lay a water main:
Then rallied all his workmen
To dump it back again

While T[omlinso]n, for gas pipes,
Picked it up galore:
Declaring he would leave it
Far better than before.

For drainage all folks trench it;
And each hundred yards at most,
Friend B[adge]r comes and delves a hole
Deep for a tramway post.

They plough it through for wires,
For B[arton]'s electric light;
They fill the openings up again,
Which is no more than right!

After running H[esketh]'s conduits,
To take the telephones;
Of course they put it back again,
Resembling stepping stones.

Oh the pavements full of furrows -
There are patches everywhere;
You stub your toes upon it,
Quite frequently you swear.
It's a very handsome pavement,
A credit to our town:
They're always diggin' of it up
Or puttin' of it down.

Patriots & Protesters

06

Two Queensland federation poets
and the Red Page Razor

John Mackenzie-Smith

Patriotic poetry experienced its halcyon days in Australia during the decade leading up to federation. It was a period of profound artistic and political activity fuelled by a surge of new-found, blatantly-flaunted nationalism.[1] In addition to the sentiments attendant on the federation campaign, there were many significant nation-binding issues and events in which the poets found their muse and expressed their literary patriotism.

Overseas, themes ranged from Australian triumphs at such hallowed English shrines as Henley and Lords to the bravery of colonial military contingents against Boer forces in South Africa. Within Australia poetic inspiration was derived from the love of the Australian environment, praise of prominent citizens, respect for pioneers and indirect support for White Australia – a poetically sanctioned experiment to create a nation with a unified British-Irish population. Although they were written in the spirit of the times, James Brunton Stephens' highly acclaimed comical poems, 'My Chinee Cook' and 'To a Black Gin', would raise more ire than laughs from multicultural Australians in the early part of the twenty-first century.[2]

The *Bulletin* was founded by John Archibald and John Haynes in 1880. It was said that 'half Australia writes it; all Australia reads it'.[3] This popular magazine exemplified and fostered the new Australian nationalism while promoting its brand of literary patriotism based on that model. Operating in parallel with the official federation movement, Australia's premier literary journal was politically and culturally Anglophobic, advocated republicanism, denounced the Boer War and advocated the White Australia policy. Most of all, it declaimed imperial federation by which Australia would in effect become a self-governing component within the British Empire, that is a federation where 'Australian nationalism was still totally integrated into Imperial patriotism'.[4] The *Bulletin* editorials argued that Australia should be left alone to enjoy its liberty and create the ideal type of society which it desired as independent people. As the 'Bushman's Bible', the *Bulletin* had no time for the imperial system that had forced such feudal imposts as the Masters & Servants Act and the squatter oligarchy upon the people who gave Australia its distinctive character.[5] Alfred George Stephens, literary editor of the *Bulletin*, proclaimed: 'Let us look at our country and its fauna and flora, its trees and mountains, through clear Australian eyes, not through biased-bleared English spectacles'.[6]

According to the *Bulletin*'s long-serving artist Norman Lindsay, that journal was the only cultural centre which Australia possessed on the eve of federation. Acting on this monopoly, its Red Page strictly created the base from which a national literature in prose and poetry flowered. The result was a school of writers committed to Australia independent of English norms. Archibald's literary hatchet man, A.G. Stephens, ruthlessly ignored or pitilessly criticised work which was inconsistent with their chauvinistic values. Their encouragement was predominantly reserved for those whose work reflected the preferred bush ethos. AGS, 'the three-initialled terror' according to Joseph Furphy, became the country's most influential, widely-read and respected literary critic. He 'guided opinion on literary value, made and unmade reputations, and published works which [became] classics'.[7]

Indeed, literary status bestowed on authors by authorities other than the *Bulletin* meant very little to Stephens as he passed his incisive eye over submitted manuscripts. Dubbed the 'Red Page hatchet' by George Essex Evans, AGS 'had no compunction about tearing to pieces' and castigating those 'who claim to be international in their approach to writing but who merely pick up London fashions'.[8] Victor Daley, Bohemian poet and member of Stephens' inner-circle, dubbed him the Rhadamanthus of the Red Page:

6.1 A.G. Stephens (JOL)

I am the Blender of the pure
Australian brand of Literature
No verse, however fine, can be
The radiant thing called Poetry
Unless it is approved by me.
I am the critic set on high;
The Red Page Rhadamanthus I.[9]

Although Scottish intellectual James Brunton Stephens had been named Australia's foremost poet following Henry Kendall's death in 1882, and Alfred Deakin proclaimed Essex Evans as Australia's national poet in 1901, the *Bulletin* preferred the relatively simply-written, Australian-authentic prose of Steele Rudd and the bush ballads of Henry Lawson and Andrew Barton Paterson. Unlike the aforementioned pair of Queensland poets whose structure was more elaborate and often modelled the style and form of current British masters such as Swinburne and Kipling, the poetry of the *Bulletin*'s proteges was viewed as fresh, original, natural, direct, British-free and it extolled the Australian landscape. Such verse conveyed clearly the sentiment that Australia, not Britain, was the poet's home and source of inspiration. Determined to encourage Australian authors to break free of the British perspective, AGS warned his readers: 'The grotesque English prejudice against things Australian, founded on no better reason than they are unlike English things, still remains to vitiate the local sense of our beauty ...'.[10]

The stormy relationship of Essex Evans and Brunton Stephens with AGS was partly the outcome of their refusal to adapt their language and sentiment to the xenophobic demands of the Bulletin School. To Essex Evans, a former Queensland Rugby Union player and prominent athlete who was sincerely intent on making a positive contribution to Australian literature, his subsequent exclusion was a bitter personal blow.[11] Unlike Brunton Stephens, this profoundly deaf literary aspirant appeared to crave that intellectual acceptance which he failed to attract as an academic underachiever at St James Collegiate School – a feeder institution for the British army and civil service.

Brunton Stephens, a product of Edinburgh University and regarded as Australia's first scholar poet, was more assertive and confident than his younger colleague; he could take or leave the *Bulletin*'s approbation, and was quite capable of calling AGS's bluff.[12] A retiring intellectual with a distaste for outdoor activities, Brunton Stephens proved to be the intellectual, literary and behavioural equal of AGS who had forged a distinguished academic record at Toowoomba Grammar School and Sydney Technical College.[13] Incongruously, Brunton Stephens was regarded as one of the Bulletin School despite his intransigence in modifying his lofty language, imperial orientation and scholarly tone to meet the obverse criteria for membership.

Brunton Stephens, proud of his Scottish birth, education and extensive travels, refused to be intimidated by AGS. He firmly resisted a basic tenet of the Bulletin School that the masters of British literature had no place in the work of Australian poets. He was unmoved by AGS's obsession to create Australian literary nationalism. On one occasion he sneered: 'Australia for the Australians, hip, hip, hooray'. On another, after AGS attempted a personal attack inferring that he lacked worldly experience, the elderly Brunton Stephens rejoined:

And wherefore should I 'soot myself and travel', mister? It is you who want to travel out of that narrow groove of modernity which is one of the most cramping of the many vogues that have come and gone in my time – the sort of thing that makes its victims ask 'What has Milton to do with Australia'? Go and steep yourself in France, Italy, Egypt and Syria, as I have done ... and you won't ask any more questions like that ... .[14]

6.2 James Brunton Stephens (JOL)

This broadside was delivered two years after two other resentful attacks in the *Bulletin* in 1898. On this occasion Brunton Stephens focused on the scholarship of AGS who scornfully declared that the Brisbane bard belonged to the sixties and seventies with Tennyson. Strongly rebutting the wild assertion that Tennyson was shallow in thought and lacked passion, the first of Brunton Stephens' resent-driven rejoinders defended the great English poet in grave language and combated the fashionable scorn of the old ways. Cecil Hadgraft, mid-twentieth century academic and Brunton Stephens' biographer, reflected, 'These two essays by Brunton Stephens were the most fruitful of literary controversy last century in all the issues of the Red Page since its inception on 29 August 1896'.[15]

The tides were turned on AGS who received a literary pasting in his own arena by an author who refused to brook his literary bullying. Essex Evans was unerringly accurate when he recalled that this intensely cultured, small Scot of slight physique was 'without a spark of jealousy or animosity to anyone ... though he could hit hard if the occasion called for it'.[16] Ultimately AGS had to acknowledge that Brunton Stephens 'always has one solid Scotch foot on the ground of fact. Sometimes he has two; even when his head is in the clouds he gets rheumatical twinges in his poetical feet from earth damp'.[17]

Having spent most of his first eight years in Queensland as a tutor at Tamrookum and Unumgar stations, the studious Brunton Stephens made no bones about his dislike for the monotony of Australian bush life and the boring conversation – just the type of author who would raise AGS's hackles. Admitting to fretting against the bush, the land of monotony, he confided to Francis Kenna: 'W was here and it was horse, horse, horse ... I literally fled the drawing room to avoid the eternal horse, horse, horse'. Nevertheless, Rosa Praed recalled that the hardened station workers refrained from ridiculing the new chum 'poet who spent hours reading Greek under a quandong tree' or was lost in the world of Euripides. 'It was curious to see how in a dim way they recognised the poet as being superior to themselves and of finer clay than the rest of us. ... they did not scoff at him, unfitted as he was, with his white hands and white cuffs and nervous shrinking from exertion'.[18]

In Scotland Brunton Stephens had written a couple of minor poems as an after-school passion, but he was driven to verse in Australia as 'relief from station life'. The narratives 'Convict once' (1871) and 'Godolphin Arabian' (1873), which received widespread critical praise, were the result of this foray into literary avoidance. AGS regarded the title of the former as the only part of the poem which was Australian. In response to friends who requested a more Australian topic, Brunton Stephens wrote the latter lengthy narrative about the ancestor of the modern thoroughbred.[19]

Knowing full well that Brunton Stephens had no intention of following or being critically bullied into implementing the *Bulletin* guidelines of literary nationalism, AGS concluded that his poems were not Australian poems, but poems about Australia. H.M. Green, writing in the 1960s, felt that there 'was a great deal of laudatory nonsense' written about 'Convict once'. Nevertheless his final assessment of Brunton Stephens' poetry confirmed that the small Scot's stance was appropriate. Despite AGS's attacks on his traditionalism, Brunton Stephens had something of value to contribute to Australian literature by being himself. Vindicating Brunton Stephens' approach, Green assessed: 'He was the first to introduce into Australia an element of broader culture, based on thought and experience of the larger world; he was also the first to introduce wit and humour into Australian poetry'.[20]

Unlike Brunton Stephens, Essex Evans was attracted to the bush life and the flora and fauna from the moment of his arrival in Queensland in 1883 as an eighteen-year-old London-born Welshman. Yearning for more intense bush experience, he joined a survey party and travelled from Warwick to the Gulf of Carpentaria within two years of disembarkation.[21] Much of his subsequent writing reflected an intimacy with the Australian landscape which he gained from that expedition. That experience especially heightened his admiration for the independent, resourceful bush workers as they eked out a living in a harsh environment. Combined with his loyalty to the British nation and its institutions, the obvious love of Australia in Essex Evans' verse earned him the title of patriotic poet of Australia.[22] His ability to blend the fond regard he held for his adopted country with loyalty to Empire provided the patriotic passion that ensured his poetry reached those heights in sentiment and language required for publication on the Red Page. Yet, his sincere, patriotic work was never considered sufficiently deserving to earn him a place beside Paterson, Lawson, Will Ogilvie and Mary Gilmour as a member of the Bulletin School. Springing to the defence of its favourite son, the loyal *Darling Downs gazette* declared: 'He was not of that school. His typical work is very far removed from the "pub and paddock jingle" variety which some people seem to think representative of Australian literary art'.[23] With more objectivity, the *Oxford companion to Australian literature* concluded nearly a century later that Essex Evans was undoubtedly a better poetic craftsman than many of his contemporaries among the bush balladists, but his popularity was mainly confined to Queensland.[24]

It was probably the Kipling-inspired verses which Essex Evans turned out literally overnight for the *Courier* to commemorate the triumphs and setbacks of the Australian contingents in South Africa which alienated the Bulletin School most of all. AGS had warned readers of the *Bulletin* of his predictable, antagonistic reaction to verse glorifying 'the war in which Australia should take no part'. 'The lion's whelps', a potboiler written in reaction to the Magersfontein reverse, depicted Australia as one of the mighty British lion's subordinate, but intensely loyal, cubs. G.K. Chesterton was as incensed in his reaction as AGS, dismissing the generally well-received verse as 'unmanly trash'. Yet favourable public opinion prevailed when Essex Evans produced 'Eland's River' in the heat of passion to commemorate the siege which proved to be Australia's most heroic action in South Africa. Received as favourably in Britain as Australia, Essex Evans' tribute had a definite *Barrack-Room Ballads* flavour about it:

> They called us to surrender, and they let their cannon lag;
> They offered us our freedom for the striking of the flag ...
> But we sent the answer in,

They could take what they could win –
We hadn't come five thousand miles to fly the coward's rag.[25]

6.3 George Essex Evans (JOL)

Nevertheless, Essex Evans was at his best writing in the genre of patriotic poetry which extolled and depicted the beauty of the adopted country which he loved and the heroic struggles of the common folk whom he admired – 'the honest toiler, the patient sufferer, the truth seeker, the nation builder'. Reginald Spencer-Browne, editor of the *Queenslander* and senior journalist for the *Brisbane courier*, readily recognised these qualities in the Toowoomba poet whom he discovered and promoted. Spencer-Browne considered that, in common with one of the fundamental qualities of the patriot, Essex Evans 'had an eye for the minor beauties of his country' which he sang with tuneful verbal melody enhanced by the skilful selection and combination of appropriate words.[26] William Archer, the eminent British literary critic at that time, agreed with Spencer-Browne's sentiments, stating that Essex Evans was at his best in description.[27] He cited an example from 'An Australian symphony':

The soft moss sleeps upon the stone
Green scrub vine traceries enthrone
The dead grey trunks ... .[28]

In poems such as 'The nation builders', from *Loraine and other verses* (1898), Essex Evans demonstrated his admiration for the endurance, tenacity and self-sacrifice of those isolated men and women who battled against overwhelming odds to open up the continent to settlement and industry. Having battled 'Thirst and fever, and famine, drought and ruin and flood' and a myriad of other formidable obstacles, such as 'the sun-cracked plain', 'the spears that redden with blood' and 'the northern jungles', the elements and land were eventually conquered, providing untold benefits for the emerging nation.[29]

In particular, 'The women of the west', from *The secret key* (1905), struck a poignant note with the English critics who lauded Essex Evans' ability to honour 'the holiness of the sacrifice; the majesty of the love which kept these women at their husbands' sides in uncomplaining loyalty which involves the loss of so much that the woman's heart holds dear' in the monotony and loneliness of the bush.[30] They left their 'vine-wreathed cottage and the mansion on the hill' to dwell in rough and ready bush dwellings such as:

... the slab-built, zinc-roofed homestead of some lately-taken run,
... the tent beside the bankment of a railway just begun.

In such isolated conditions they loyally endured without recognition 'while the red sun robs their beauty':

For them no trumpet sounds a call, no poet plies his arts –
They only hear the beating of their gallant, loving hearts,

But they have sung with silent lives the song all songs above –
The holiness of sacrifice, the dignity of love.[31]

A century later Michael Ackland, Monash University academic and specialist in nineteenth century Australian literature, was more sceptical of such standard critical reactions. He discerned strong sexist overtones in this poem. While the long list of sufferings appeared to indicate feminine willingness to undergo privation and did in fact give 'women their due in the frontier struggle, [the poem really] assured their continued subjugation' to male designs.[32]

The *Repentance of Magdelin Despar* (1891) and *Loraine* (1898), Essex Evans' two book-length narratives, received high critical acclaim. The *Australasian critic* of May 1891 considered the former to rival the work of Adam Lindsay Gordon, being the very best volume of verse by an author that had been published for many a year. According to this journal Essex Evans' work fulfilled many of the criteria which the *Bulletin* required of aspiring poets. Much of *Magdelin Despar* gave voice to energetic Australian life and vividly portrayed 'our bright sun and cloudless deep blue skies'.[33]

Indeed, the *Spectator* in London recognised within Essex Evans' poetry a form of artistry which was 'purely and distinctly Australian'. While praising the vividness and individuality of the description, this English journal recognised the skilful hand of the artist with 'vital feeling' for the nuances of Australian scenery:[34]

The grey gums by the lonely creek
The star-crowned height,
The wind-swept plain, the dim blue peak,
The solitude near and far
Around the camp-fire's tiny star,
The horse-bell's melody remote,
The curlew's melancholy note
Across the night.

The Age also found echoes of Gordon in *Magdelin Despar*, albeit with a Kipling influence.[35] While this journal too expressed admiration for his description of Australian scenery and seasons in *Loraine and other verses,* the *Melbourne punch* declared the volume to be a decided acquisition to Australian literature. It was asserted that such vivid poetry put the author in the same rank as Gordon, Kendall and Brunton Stephens.[36] Predictably Spencer Browne's review in the *Courier* was also favourable, praising Essex Evans' powerful description of scenery.[37]

Such positive feedback renewed Essex Evans' vow to give of his very best to Australian literature. He regarded Spencer Browne's critique as 'real criticism that helps towards improvement in art'. Feeling 'strong for future work', Essex Evans offered his reaction to negative criticism, the type of which AGS was mercilessly capable, the kind he was to receive at the beginning of 1901. 'The style of review that tears everything to shreds is easy writing and also has the effect of tearing all enthusiasm out of a man's heart'.[38]

A.G. Stephens, with a mind 'sharpened by contact with the best contemporary writing in England and France', valued originality and simplicity above the conventional and dense. His judgement was sound, friendship never entering into the realm of literary review.[39] According to H.A. Kellow, an Australian critic who took a fresh look at Essex Evans' poetry in 1930, AGS may not have been unreasonable in his criticism of the Toowoomba bard's work. Kellow considered that there was a lack of freshness of thought in Essex Evans' poetry, lack of originality and too frequent use of the works of well-known poets such as Brunton Stephens, Swinburne and Kipling as models. As a close friend, admirer and veritable disciple of Brunton Stephens, it is not unexpected that Essex Evans transparently reflected his influence. Nevertheless, it was felt this patterning was performed with 'graceful skill'. Importantly, the subject matter and language were original. However, unlike Brunton Stephens' complex narratives, which reflected scholarship and freshness in thought, Kellow considered, with thankful relief, that Essex Evans' poems were neither bookish nor overlaid with the polysyllabic ornamentation which were the hallmark of his mentor.[40]

The influential patriotic poetry and popular anthems composed by these two Queenslanders, forecasting and advocating the union of the Australian colonies, proved to be important components in the repertoire of some of the most eminent of the statesmen who led the federation campaign. Specifically, the verse of Brunton Stephens and Essex Evans was recited or sung at strategic junctures during large public meetings to arouse chauvinistic emotions. As such, they substantially contributed to the campaign, especially the desperate attempt to persuade the recalcitrant colonies of Queensland and Western Australia to belatedly enter the national fold.[41]

With political, cultural and military conditions propitious for national union, Sir Henry Parkes quoted one significant stanza of Brunton Stephens' 'Dominion of Australia – a forecast' during his speech at Tenterfield in October 1889. Having discussed his plans for federation with the Queensland premier, Parkes delivered a speech on the NSW-Queensland border which arguably 'kick-started' the national campaign to that end. His poetic diversion powerfully reinforced his argument that the time had arisen for the creation of an Australian constitution and national parliament.[42]

In the full poem, Brunton Stephens argued the case for federation by sustained simile. He proposed that beneath the surface of Australian life a huge swell of nationalism, similar to an unseen, underground river, was flowing. This surge would inexorably swell to such a degree that the colonies would be launched dramatically into federation. Transcending colonial rivalries and factions, Brunton Stephens' ode 'lifted the discussion to ... lofty idealism'. Having noted that the union was 'not yet', he predicted in 1877 that 'She is nigh'. Parkes, estimating that 1889 was the time to act and with some light-hearted encouragement from the New South Wales Governor Lord Carrington, quoted to great effect:

Not yet her day. How long 'not yet'?
There comes a flash of violet!
And heavenward faces all aflame
With sanguine imminence of morn
Wait but the sun-kiss to proclaim
The day of the Dominion born.[43]

Significantly Parkes chose to quote from this 1877 poem rather than a more recent and optimistic work. Convinced that the ideal of federation was achievable and imminent, Brunton Stephens had followed up 'The Dominion of Australia' with 'The Dominion' in 1883. He asked what was holding back the colonies, the seven stars which would form the coronet of the personified 'Ideal', from uniting politically and economically. Amidst the group of stanzas in which the attributes of each colony, 'sisters seven', are described, Queensland is designated 'the youngest and the fair; First discern and first to dare'.[44]

This work was obviously inspired by the early initiative of Premier Griffith. In 1883 he proposed the establishment of a federal council – the seminal body which provided the colonies with limited federal legislative experience.[45]

When the federation campaign reached its zenith in the late 1890s, both of Queensland's pre-eminent poets penned the words to spurious national anthems which proved to be powerful means of arousing national sentiment. Brunton Stephens wrote the 'Australian Anthem', with music composed by J. Summers, which began 'Maker of earth and sea, What shall we render thee All things are thine!' and reached its peak at the stirring conclusion of the penultimate verse:

Let us united stand,
One great Australian band
Heart to heart, hand in hand,
Heart and hand thine.[46]

In 1899 Essex Evans produced 'A federal song', music composed by George Sampson. Paying tribute to Brunton Stephens who first raised the federation issue in verse, Essex Evans' words evoked rousing emotional responses from various massed audiences throughout Australia, apparently clinching the orators' arguments in favour of federation:

All the greyness of the dawning, all the mists are over-past,
In the glory of the morning we shall see Her face at last.
He who sang, 'She yet shall be,'
He shall hail her, crowned and free!
Could we break the land asunder God has girdled with the Sea!
For the flag is floating o'er us,
And the star of Hope before us,
From the desert to the ocean, brothers lift the mighty chorus
For Australian Unity'.[47]

Alfred Deakin enthusiastically acknowledged that the Australian people readily took to this patriotic song which produced positive effects in the campaign and brought the late-comers from Queensland and Western Australia into the fold. At the final, overflowing federal meeting held at Perth on the eve of that colony's referendum, the 'Federal song' was sung with fervour as the Australian flag was unfurled. The *Review of reviews* reported on 15 August 1900 that the song struck an emotional chord with the western audience: They 'cheered the words of the Queensland poet again and again, and those that took part in the demonstration will not soon forget it'.[48]

Brunton Stephens' anthem was launched under similar conditions at the corresponding meeting on the eve of Queensland's referendum – eleven months earlier on 1 September 1899. It produced similar demonstrations of 'wild enthusiasm'. Regrettably this joyous zeal was dampened by the ire of Brisbane's anti-federation mob screaming, 'Queensland for the Queenslanders' as it assaulted Edmund Barton, soon to become Australia's first prime minister.[49]

A supplement to the *Brisbane courier* on 2 September 1899 made a final play for a successful outcome of the referendum to be held on the following day. Brunton Stephens' 'A forecast' and Essex Evans' 'A federal song' were prominently featured along with rousing articles by Deakin and the premiers of Queensland, NSW and Victoria urging an overwhelming 'yes' vote. The former proclaimed:

> We are of one stock and enjoy one inheritance. The history we have yet to make must be one also. We can only make history worthy of our sires and ourselves when we make so as one Nation in one Commonwealth.[50]

Two days later the positive result of the referendum was celebrated in the *Brisbane courier*. Spencer-Browne wrote the leading article which noted the flags that were flying from many buildings, particularly the federal flag – the white ensign with the blue bars and stars of Australia. The sea of upturned faces waving hats, sticks, umbrellas and handkerchiefs below the balcony of the Courier Building reacted enthusiastically to speeches by Barton, Robert Philp and other dignitaries with a mixture of victory cheers and disapproving hoots. In all, it was universally agreed by the winners that this federal victory did not merely belong to Queensland but to Australia. Towards the end of his article, Spencer-Browne claimed: 'In many hearts on Saturday night the swing of Essex Evans' splendid verse was throbbing':

To the North of the seas of summer, where the pearl flotillas swim.
To East where the axe is ringing in the heart of the ranges grim.

'Tis war and stress with never a pause to mourn for a stout heart gone
Till the souls of the Nation Builders shall know that their work is done.[51]

When federation became a reality and 'the golden hope, of which Essex Evans sang, had been realised' on 1 January 1901, Spencer-Browne was once more constrained to intone his protege's sentiments from 'The nation builders':

> ... the land that lies like a giant asleep shall wake in the victory won,
> And the heart of the Nation Builders shall know that their work is done!

6.4 Major R. Spencer-Browne (JOL)

Proclaiming that the Australian-born and those originating from other countries were thenceforth native-born, Spencer-Browne reiterated Brunton Stephens' sentiments that the nation's destiny was thereafter in their hands. The 'crimson thread of kinship' in which the long-deceased Parkes had put his trust had triumphed.[52]

Other newspapers throughout Australia also published Brunton Stephens' 'Fulfilment' which applauded the achievement of federation, honoured Australia's pioneers, paid fealty to Queen Victoria and counselled that the future of the nation would require the commitment and hard work of all Australians:

> The Charter's read; the rites are o'er;
> The trumpet's blare and cannon's roar
> Are silent, and the flags are furled;
> But not so ends the task to build
> Into the fabric of the world
> The substance of our hope fulfilled.[53]

Also prominently featured in the *Courier* was Essex Evans' 'Commonwealth ode', the winning entry in a nation-wide competition sponsored by the NSW government for such a poem to suitably celebrate federation. Chris Tiffin has provided a precis of the triumphant poem:

> Australia is depicted as a sleeping virgin at dawn about to be kissed awake by the sun of progress. She is surrounded by the sea. She is empty, memoryless and unproductive, but she has enormous natural beauties and resources. As she is awakened into productivity, each of the constituent elements (the Colonies) takes on identifying emblems based on the resources for commerce they possess.[54]

Queensland, one of the 'maidens linked in love', is personified as a 'Sun-maid in whose veins For ever burns the tropic fire'. Like Brunton Stephens, Essex Evans saluted and invoked the spirits of the pioneers 'Who fought and dared, who toiled and bled, That this might be – '. However, ignoring the history of the violent dispossession of Australia's indigenes, Essex Evans erroneously claimed that the new nation 'was not won by blood'.[55]

Today feminist criticism of such federation poetry has focused on the male poets' predilection to 'encode all relationships within the existing discourse of patriarchal gender relations', that is the sleeping virgin. In such poetry it is claimed that the commonplace depiction of the new state of Australia as a woman threatens the male libido and the 'challenge is articulated in terms [which] facilitate male bonding against the predatory female and against the land'. The new state, allegorical woman, as ordained by men with a common cause, is viewed as being purely male-oriented, giving promise of a 'paradisal home for other men worthy of sharing the vision'.[56]

Such censure is mild compared with the adverse reaction which the ode evoked from A.G. Stephens on the Red Page in the *Bulletin's* first edition for 1901. AGS started by pouring scorn upon the organisation of the competition by Premier William Lyne who could not 'write or speak ten original lines'. He then turned his rapier pen upon the qualifications and competence of the non-literary judges to perform their important adjudication in such a significant literary contest. Instead of the prominent public figures who comprised the panel, AGS argued that the panel should have been comprised established poets of the calibre of Brunton Stephens, Victor Daley and Chris Brennan 'whose literary brains are deservedly respected'.

AGS then focused his vitriol on the winning poet and his apparently unsatisfactory ode. Conceding that Essex Evans was 'a fine fellow' who wrote excellent verse but not inspiring poetry, he severely criticised his lack of originality:

> Not one new phrase, not one subtle cadence, not one Essex Evans-born idea. 'Awake! Arise!' - an opening so banal that even Henry Lawson parodied it. The time-worn 'dawn' metaphor ... and touch which suggests at once Brunton Stephens's 'Dominion of Australia'.

He then went on to mock the neat pigeonholes into which the various colonies were slotted and condemned the conclusion which too closely resembled Kipling's 'Recessional' (1897). Finally, AGS dismissed the ode as not worthy of the prize, being 'a cento of other people's words and thoughts ...'.[57]

However, the matter did not lie there; the 'Red Page hatchet' sensed there was impropriety afoot. Within a fortnight of this literary attack, the *Bulletin* strongly inferred that Essex Evans had influenced the judges' decision and he had received unfair advantage. No doubt AG Stephens' reaction would have been more volcanic if he had known that Deakin, himself a dabbler in poetry, was also involved in an advisory capacity.

It was claimed on 19 January that the judges had selected Essex Evans' ode before the closing date and asked him to make three amendments before they declared the winner. Suspicions were aroused when it appeared that Essex Evans apparently anticipated the demands of the judges; he had forwarded a second copy of the poem with the identical improvements as officially requested! Heavy with insinuation, the *Bulletin* suggested that he might well have been a thought-reader as well as a poet.[58]

Essex Evans wrote to Deakin, also of Welsh lineage, on 4 October 1900, when the ode competition was merely a rumour. He reminded Deakin that the 'Federal Song' had materially influenced the Queensland and Western Australian federation campaigns and praised Barton's and Deakin's unstinting labours to achieve nationhood. He also commented upon Deakin's favourable reaction to *Loraine*, before asking for an opinion on his ode. Essex Evans further stated that at that juncture he was undecided whether to enter the competition or to immediately publish the poem which designedly ignored the Empire, Boer War and Queen. He informed Deakin that Brunton Stephens had already made up his mind, declining to enter the mooted competition. He deemed that such a contest was 'too akin to calling tenders to appeal to one's taste'.[59]

Essex Evans' reply on 10 October to a swift response from Deakin indicated that the latter indeed made suggestions, to which the former mostly complied. J.A. La Nauze, one of Deakin's biographers, indicated that his sympathy was prompted by his own unrealised aspirations as a poet.[60] Anticipating the imminent release of one of Kipling's new poems and frustrated at the procrastination of the NSW government, Essex Evans revealed that he had decided to publish the ode in the Melbourne *Argus,* 'one of the best newspapers in the world'. Uppermost in his mind was his resolve to avoid the charge of plagiarising of Kipling's most recent verse which was about to be published. Requesting Deakin to act on his behalf and keeping open the possibility of entering the competition, Essex Evans gave instruction that the editor seal the poem in an envelope until 1 January 1901 if the *Argus* decided not to publish his verse. Possibly playing on the legendary inter-city rivalry, Essex Evans informed Deakin that he would send the ode to Sydney newspapers if the Melbourne journal rejected it.[61]

6.5 George Essex Evans (JOL)

Ten days later the ode was published in the *Argus*. It was noted beneath the poem that although the ode was written for 1 January, the author decided to publish it prematurely. Unknown to Essex Evans, this version was subsequently extracted from the *Argus* by a person unknown and submitted when the NSW government eventually threw open the nation-wide competition.

On 23 March 1905 Essex Evans made the first of his conciliatory gestures towards 'Stephens of the Red Page [who] has been for years my inveterate literary foe'.[62] He was deeply touched that AGS should think that 'An Australian symphony' was worthy of being included in an anthology of Australian poetry that he was compiling. Essex Evans admitted that his bête noire had been entitled to his opinion over the years, but it was Stephens' perceived attempts to 'block' his work that vexed him most of all. Benevolently admitting that he had misjudged AGS, he interpreted his inclusion as evidence that his suspicions had been misplaced.[63] Perhaps Essex Evans had been too generous and forgiving as his attempts to compile a similar anthology were indeed blocked three and a half years previously. At that time the *Bulletin* refused him permission to publish some of the better poems which graced the Red Page over the previous years.[64] Climbing down from years of affront, Essex Evans let bygones be bygones. Declining to become bitter in this matter or even petulantly refusing A.G. Stephens' publication rights of 'An Australian symphony', this staunch Anglican conceded that his bitter disappointment was then 'ancient history'.

One year later, Essex Evans again raised the subject of his misunderstanding with AGS, and he attempted to clear up the suspicion which surrounded his victory in the ode contest. Opening his letter with 'Life is too short for small feuds', Essex Evans stated that he 'honestly thought' that he had been unfairly treated by the *Bulletin* although he did not mind the adverse criticism heaped upon him. Acknowledging that AGS gave his honest opinion, he reversed his earlier outburst on adverse literary reviews with which he had regaled Spencer-Browne. Now he accepted that adverse criticism 'is the best thing that can happen to an author' and should not affect personal relations. Once more he appeared to be too contrite in order to clinch Stephens' perceived peace offers.[65] The conciliatory gesture on this occasion was a copy of the verse of the late Victor Daley whom Essex Evans had assisted by financial contribution during the Irish poet's final illness.[66]

Dealing with the insinuation that he had been in collusion with the judges of the Constitutional Ode contest, Essex Evans swore that he knew none of them and that only one ode had been sent in by him. According to Essex Evans, an unknown person had submitted the *Argus* version and Essex Evans independently entered the improved version – the last ode that was received. The former version was declared the winner, provisional on the author making some small alterations. It was claimed that there was no 'double-dealing' as the judges eventually located Essex Evans' own entry, incongruously complete with the required corrections after the request for amendments was made.

Finally, from Essex Evans' point of view, the hatchet was buried. He declared:

> So let us end the petty feuds for which no doubt I am partly to blame. I want you to get it out of your head that I am sore about adverse criticism. I admire the work you have done for Australia and hope you will be long spared to continue it.[67]

A.G. Stephens was destined to continue his valuable work for Australian literature, but Essex Evans had merely three more years of painful life left to him before dying prematurely of post-operational complications in November 1909. His friend and mentor, James Brunton Stephens, predeceased him by seven years, living long enough to see federation achieved. Essex Evans' admiration for Brunton Stephens was enshrined in verse:

> The gentle heart that hated wrong,
> The courage that all ills withstood,
> he seeing eye, the mighty song
> That stirred us into Nationhood,
> Have passed. What garlands can be spread?
> The Prince of Courtesy is dead.[68]

While Essex Evans appears to have received no similar poetic tributes, the *South Wales daily news* in Cardiff, the *Spectator* in London, Toowoomba's *Darling Downs gazette* and the *Brisbane courier* were among the many newspapers which ran extensive laudatory obituaries. An avowed imperialist, he would have been elated by the tribute in the former journal which proudly stated that the brilliant son of Wales, who had made his home for the greater part of his too-short life in Queensland, would earn a permanent place amongst the Australian poets.

> With all the fervour of the Celt, he threw himself into the life of his far-off home. The solitude of the bush, the vigorous life of the colony abounding in material prosperity and hope for the future, the Imperial relations between the Australian Colonies and the Mother Country, these were the themes which inspired his muse.[69]

Spencer-Browne, fellow-poet and Australian military hero, saw beyond the imperialism that made Essex Evans unpopular with that group of the Australian literati who advocated literary nationalism. Despite their reservations, Spencer-Browne declared him to be a true Australian patriot whose optimistic poetry would live on:

> That he held in his heart the people of this land, entering into their struggles, admiring their heroisms ... . He was a patriot poet. ... For the honest toiler, the patient sufferer, the truth seeker, the nation builder, there is in his pages a wealth of inspiration.[70]

The final assessment of AG Stephens, who left the *Bulletin* in a pique in 1906, is unrecorded. However, Australia's second prime minister accorded Essex Evans the patriotic tribute which he was denied by the Red Page Rhadamanthus. To the leader of the movement which was the very manifestation of real Australian nationalism, Essex Evans was heralded as Australia's national poet 'whose patriotic song stirred her people profoundly in the arduous campaign for union'.[71]

But AGS's opinion when he locked horns with Brunton Stephens 102 years ago has proved to be portentous and possibly the last word when the poetry of Queensland's two patriotic poets is evaluated early in the twenty-first century. For the most part, their poetry has not been well received by subsequent generations of Australians. It is only the current focus on the centenary of federation that has revealed for transitory admiration the considerable but forgotten role that their muse played in the public process that forged the commonwealth. A search in a contemporary Australian anthology will probably unearth either Essex Evans' 'Nation builders' or 'Women of the west', but the remainder of their poetry is probably confined to academic examination in elective poetry courses within university English departments. Independently holding the same opinion as AGS whose faith in Lawson, Rudd and Barton Paterson appears vindicated, the distinguished late-twentieth century poet Judith Wright concluded that Brunton Stephens and Essex Evans were 'both ... highly-conventional, late Tennysonian romantics and neither has worn well'.[72]

The poetry of Brunton Stephens and Essex Evans may well have been unpopular with the late twentieth century reading public and condemned by its thought police. These men of letters, whose work was highly acclaimed in sophisticated Britain, were certainly no strangers to controversy in their time. According to the chauvinistic criteria of the influential *Bulletin* at the turn of the century, their work was assuredly politically incorrect in form, content and allegiance. However, they could never have anticipated the proliferation of the 'linguistic trip-cords' which severely restrain the cognitive, expressive and creative processes of modern authors.

While they simply reflected the values, sentiments and prejudices of their era and are now unquestionably out of fashion, this should not detract from their historical significance. In their day, their rousing anthems and inspiring poems were strategically important as motivational and celebratory tools in the hands of those who successfully persuaded recalcitrant individuals and colonies to support the birth of the Australian nation. Appreciated for their significant contributions to the pro-federation campaign, Brunton Stephens and Essex Evans, particularly the latter, were mentioned in despatches by those who were prominent in the front line. If justice be done, this pair of presently passé poets must at least retain the well-deserved footnote which they currently enjoy in the annals of Australian history.

07 Brisbane
at Federation : 1899-1902

Raymond Evans

Brisbane has always evaded easy historical categorisation. Temporally, it has been something of a shape-changer. Yet each time researchers appear to have pinned down its *Zeitgeist*, it escapes mercury-like through the fingers. Like a chameleon it assumes different colours and aspects. It is probably the world's only modern city which does not know its exact date of European inception; and its overall historical contours have remained shadowy and evasive. Weatherboard towns imply a fugitive sense of historical impermanency, it would seem.

'What a place!' David Malouf's Johnno would snarl in the late 1940s exasperated by the dust and the packed heat: 'This must be the bloody arsehole of the universe!' And Malouf, as narrator, even though loving the place a little more, had to admit:

> ... it was difficult to see how anything could be made of Brisbane. It was so shabby and makeshift ... . Nothing seemed permanent here. Brisbane was a huge shanty town set down in the middle of nowhere ... . It wouldn't have surprised anyone, I think, to wake up one morning and find that Brisbane too had died overnight. Its corrugated iron sold off for scrap. The weatherboard houses would rot in the damp ... . Animals would nest in upturned water-tanks.
>
> And who, Johnno asked, would know the difference. Brisbane was nothing; a city that blew neither hot nor cold, a place where nothing happened, and where nothing ever would happen, because it had no soul. People suffered here without significance. It was too mediocre even to be a province of hell. ... A place where poetry could never occur.

But then, Malouf adds, in a paragraph all to itself, the word 'perhaps ...'.[1]

Writing about Brisbane four decades earlier and setting his novel *The blood vote* in the years of the First World War, Jack Lindsay provided a similar sense of a sleepy passionless place, converging always towards historical anticlimax. Although the rag-tag Brisbane bunch of socialists and 'wobblies' try to invoke the conscription debate of 1917 as 'a ferocious struggle of murder and it was being waged here, here ... in this quiet street of shops with subdued lights and advertised good ... while the lovers whispered among the glasscases', in the end nothing seems to come of it: 'On the twentieth November 1917 federal police were posted at the Brisbane voting booths to show that the militarists considered Brisbane the heart of the resistance. But there was no violence ...'.[2]

The author misses entirely here the drama of Brisbane verging closely upon outright civil war at this juncture. ... It being such a soulless, passionless place, how could such a thing possibly happen?[3]

When Ron Lawson reconstructed Brisbane of the 1890s in his 1973 urban history, a similar presentiment of passivity, unanimity and torpor seemed to mould the contours of his massive study. His index carries no entries on struggle or conflict and the only entry under 'Race' refers to high attendances at Eagle Farm, Ascot and Albion Park. Although he begins, provocatively enough, by seeing Brisbane as 'the city from which the most rapid advances in the growth of mass trade unionism were organised' and 'the capital of the colony where the most bitter strikes took place' – the place where 'the most extreme labour party in the colonies' confronted the 'most conservative government' – these factors seem to account for little or nothing in his final summation of Brisbane at federation as a place of 'prevailing social harmony' where 'cohesion' ruled.[4]

Brisbane society represented, Lawson concluded, 'a hierarchy of closely adjacent status positions with no obvious breaks' which left no room for class conflict. Workers 'had reason to be fairly content with their lot' while their employers, although 'jealous of their privileges ... readily accepted that everyone would enjoy a measure of material well being'. Thus the frequent contemporary press allusion – from both conservative and labour organs to 'class war' were to Lawson merely chimerical. The great strikes of the 1890s were dismissed in one short sentence. The 'lower classes' he writes, 'were content to work within the structure of society as it stood and so did not contest the common middle-class values which underlay it'. In fact many 'looked to the middle class as their "reference group"' and those who did not were 'usually innocuous hedonists devoted to liquor and gambling rather than political revolutionaries'.[5]

Lawson's federation Brisbane is 'fluid', with 'upward occupational mobility' common. 'Religious sectarianism' is no threat here. Gender and race struggle are not even considered. Class struggle is utterly dismissed. Looking back on this book from today's vantage point, it now appears as a predictable Cold War product, a study which underscores Australia's exceptionalism as a place of peace, sanctity, equality and fairness. Indeed, Bill Thorpe's critique of 1987 uncovered its fundamental weakness – a theoretical misreading and selective misquoting of Max Weber and T.B. Bottomore in order to unfairly debunk Marxian analysis.[6]

Since then the debate about Brisbane and social conflict has lain fairly dormant though it has been raised recently, though somewhat tangentially, by Stephen Stockwell in an article called 'Wonderful progress: Alternative currents in colonial Brisbane'. In this piece, Stockwell develops a paradigm of 'contradictory tendencies'_in the history of the capital – the mainstream bodies marching under the banner of 'progress' confronting various cultures of resistance – racial, class-based, generational and environmental. This interpretive frame allows space for various countervailing tendencies to co-exist in parallel proximity. For instance, Stockwell talks of 'quirky, impromptu and "close to nature" lifestyles that give rise to the perception that Brisbane is different from other Australian cities'. Quoting Thea Astley, he mentions, 'An oddly distorted sense of space and distance, a dilated sense of time, a sense of being "on the edge" and a violent antithesis between contrarieties thrown together – town and country, modern and primitive, learning and ignorance'.

It is this sense of contrariety and exaggerated social atmospherics which draws him – as it draws me – towards recurring 'public displays of antipathy'. He mentions the 1912 Tramway Strike, the 1949 St Patrick's Day conflict, the rock-and-roll riots of the 1950s, the student demonstrations of the 1960s, the street marches of the 1970s and even the Sandgate Handicap riot of the 1880s.[7]

To these 'recurring public displays' should be added the 1866 Bread and Blood riots, the 1888 Anti-Chinese riots – the most serious racial rioting on the eastern coastline at that time – the Brisbane anti-conscription riots of the First World War, the Red Flag riots of 1919 and the most serious urban ethnic rioting of this era – the Pineapple Rebellion of 1939, when a group of disgruntled Social Credit farmers kidnapped the entire Queensland cabinet in Parliament House – and, of course, the Battle of Brisbane in 1942, where one man was killed and several dozen injured in successive nights of disorder.[8]

What does this parallel history of disorderliness and struggle mean; and how does it relate to the central focus of this paper – the Brisbane fin de siècle social dis/order?

One dominant historical strand presents this city as being 'from its earliest days a quiet and boring town ... a very law abiding community', and Lawson's gently graded social order, where dullness was the price paid for tranquillity in this drowsy overgrown country township, forms a central thread to this paradigm.[9]

Evidence of disorder, however, feeds into a contradictory historiographical strand which insists that the Queensland capital possessed its seamier side, its wilder side, its more passionate, articulate side. It was the place that gave birth to William Lane's iconoclasm and Francis Adams' *Songs of the army of the night*:

But rise and join us...
Beside the roadways, rise
Fill up the ranks! What shimmers there so bright?
The Bayonets of the Army of the Night.

– a paean to class warfare written in Rosalie in the late 1880s. It provided the cultural genesis for Vere Gordon Childe's *How Labour governs*, Clem Christisons's *Meanjin* and the Saints' *I'm stranded*, the first global punk anthem. It is the place, according to Kevin Lingard, where 'larrikinism has continued well after its demise elsewhere'. And it is also, according to cultural commentator R. Harley, 'a place of extremes ... a place of risk'.[10]

When I attempted to address this historical paradox in *The Red Flag riots* (1988), I observed that: '... from its convict roots to its present day conservation, land rights, civil liberation and trade union struggles, [Brisbane] grew in conflict and travail as well as its dusty urban sprawl ...'.[11]

How did this allegedly 'classless' town of the nineties play host in 1899 to the world's first Labor government and then in 1912 to Australia's – and possibly the world's – first General Strike? How did this purportedly law-abiding, 'homogeneous' community produce the savagely xenophobic, loyalist rioting of 1919 much as it had the worst anti-Chinese violence on the eastern sea-board in 1888? Do we truly stand upon a tranquil urban plain to witness these sudden tumults? Is the tumult perhaps, a mirage? Or is the plain in reality simply a shaky historical paradigm which the evidence of tumult interrogates and, ultimately, disowns? In this paper these questions are applied more closely to Brisbane at federation and to certain public behaviours of Brisbane's citizens between the years 1899 and 1902.

At first sight, the federation era does not appear as fertile ground for sighting of overt conflict. Although John Hirst in his recent study of the making of the Australian Commonwealth, *The sentimental nation*, refers in passing to the Republican riots of 1887, the anti-Chinese violence of 1888, general assaults against Aboriginal people and the tumult of the Great Strikes between 1890 and 1894, he emphasises that federation was the product of 'a peaceful democratic movement'. Australian society was 'pristine, harmonious and progressive'. Australians congregated under their 'thin, tin cracking roofs ... drinking tea as a sandhill drinks water'. 'Australia enjoyed its peace ... free from old world rivalries and wars'.[12]

The wave of largely execrable poetry which washed in federation celebrated this passivity. Banjo Paterson wrote:

we have no songs of strife
Of bloodshed reddening the land,

Queensland poet George Essex Evans described the new commonwealth as:

Free born of Nations, Virgin white,
Not won by blood nor ringed by steel ...

And Ashgrove State School headmaster, James Brunton Stephens, in one of the better federation poems, wrote of how the gathering force of Common Will would

... hide our barren feuds in bloom
Till, all our sundering lines with love o'ergrown,
Our bounds shall be the girdling seas alone ...

'I think that we are free from any race antipathy', added Henry Bourne Higgins for good measure.[13]

So the overall cultural impression – and the common historical consensus – is that across the colonies federation and tranquillity went virtually hand in hand. And so it did, it would seem, everywhere. Everywhere that is, besides Brisbane. Examination of a number of episodes occurring in turn of the century Brisbane is clearly warranted.

On the eve of the Queensland Federation Referendum of 2 September 1899, two gatherings, pro- and anti-union clashed violently in the city centre. At the Centennial Hall in Adelaide Street, eminent political and social leaders, headed by Premier James Dickson and Robert Philip, and including T.A. Ryan, the later architect of Anzac Day, gathered to hear addresses by visiting dignitaries, Edmund Barton and J.S. Larke, the Canadian Commissioner. The crammed meeting was extremely enthusiastic and a huge overflow audience of several thousands filled the streets outside.

This overflow crowd was soon engaging in heated clashes with large numbers of anti-federalists, the 'grass in Queen St' crowd, who had organised a counter-demonstration on the town hall reserve. Processions of thousands of people from the suburbs, led by brass bands and carrying oil torchlights, placards and union jacks on long poles began arriving, filling the reserve, where four speakers' platforms on the backs of lorries had been set up, and crowding the whole of Albert Street, between Ann and Adelaide streets. People were 'crushed together till there was scarce breathing room', the *Brisbane courier* wrote.

As the anti-federalists began to air their case, Barton's overflow audience began to interject, hooting and groaning, and soon violence erupted:

> No fewer than four free fights took place, on one occasion as many as forty combatants being counted. Every now and again an anti-federal flag was torn to pieces .... .

The jeering, hooting and cheering became cacophonous:

> Sometimes a section of a band had become partially demented and would march in and out of the crowd blowing noisily with much drum accompaniment. Then the speakers would wave their hats and fill up the interval with cheering.

One fracas occurred around a rostrum set up in Market Place which was intended for Barton to address the federalists in the street. When a Mr Scott mounted this platform to harangue the crowd, he was first assaulted with missiles and then physically attacked. The lorry was rushed and overturned. 'Mob rule succeeded', the *Courier* noted. 'And the proceedings turned into a pandemonium'.

About an hour into the proceedings, Barton emerged from Centennial Hall to address the pro-union crowd only to find that 'the federal speaking stand had been destroyed'. As he made his way through the throng accompanied by a Mr Farrell he was recognised:

> A crowd of boys began to call out my name, [he later stated]. This attracted a crowd ... who proceeded to crush us.

Barton had determined to address the rally from the balcony of the Albert Hotel but the crowd intervened. The *Courier* wrote:

> The mob were not satisfied until they had assaulted Mr Barton and caused a scene which will ... create such a revulsion of feeling in the colony as will certainly not profit the anti-federal cause. Hundreds of men and boys behaved like many wild animals ... Mr Barton was pushed and jostled in a way that has never happened to a visitor before.

According to Barton himself:

> The crowd endeavoured to prevent us [but] I am happy to say my weight told. When we reached the footpath ... we were pushed and shoved. I faced around and showed fight, demanding to be met face to face ... but as soon as I turned my back the attacks were renewed ... I managed to get inside the hotel, having first returned a blow.

Barton then took refuge inside as hundreds of his assailants rushed the doors. One unfortunate gentleman who did appear on the upper balcony, being mistaken for the future prime minister, was pelted with rotten eggs.

When Barton attempted later to return to Centennial Hall, he was again pursued. 'I felt the stroke of a pebble or something of that sort', he testified, 'but beyond that I did not suffer'. The crowd, however, had surged into the corridor behind him and a plain-clothes detective had to effect his escape.

Inside the meeting hall, the Canadian Commissioner informed the audience of Barton's mobbing to cries of shame, adding, '... men have got so frightened for their cause they have lost their reason ... Mr Barton ... will suffer more than a few blows or bruises to see the cause succeed'.

Barton by this time had entered a cab in Edward Street and made his escape; but his assailants, thinking he had returned to the Albert Hotel, again rushed its doors and were dispersed by police. The demonstration did not end until midnight, members declaring 'they would wait for Barton if it were till morning'.

The following day, Queensland declared narrowly for federation as Brisbane itself voted substantially against it. That evening Barton and Dickson addressed a huge concourse outside the Courier Building in Queen Street. Some 'ancient eggs' were again thrown; some fist fights occurred and hardly a word of the speeches could be heard above the din. *Progress* journal commented:

> Hats, sticks, umbrellas and handkerchiefs were waving in the air; cheers, shrieks, yells, frantic and unrestrained applause rent the heavens – the great mass of humanity swelled and surged like one enormous living body.[14]

But the principal excitement of this period was not directed towards the federal question at all, but rather towards the cause of the new nation's involvement in the Boer War. Queensland had been the first colony in the Empire to offer troops – even before the fighting had actually broken out – and by early 1900, the jingoistic spirit was running rampant. The war became another cause for passionate displays in the capital.

Commenting intimately upon this in April 1900, Judge William Shand wrote in a letter home to Baron Thomas Farrah:

> ...one can't help being struck by the genuine outburst of loyalty to the Motherland which the war has exploded ... based upon a real foundation of social unity ... it has been a most pleasant surprise to me.
>
> The most patriotic man in Brisbane is a Chemist who keeps a shop [in Queen Street] which is now popularly known as the War Office. ... when things are bad ... he will not speak and only wave his arms helplessly as the turtle manipulates its flippers. But if he is hurrying to and fro with the tails of a long frock coat waving in the breeze – all will be well ... He has been known to weep real tears of joy and real tears of sorrow ... in fact the man is a raving lunatic from sheer patriotism. But he prospers The community will only buy from patriots.

Shand here alluded to the darker side of loyalism which had begun to boycott alleged pro-Boers:

> Another man ... keeps a large restaurant in the same street and before the war no more a popular and prosperous caterer was to be found in Brisbane ... But also Germany claims him as a son and his name is Eschen Hagen. What wonder then that rumours should ascribe disloyal sentiments to him ... Who cares whether it be true or false, folks (especially colonial folks) being wonderfully similar to overgrown children?
>
> He protests his innocence through the medium of the public press. He hangs his shop with Union Jacks whenever any little British success seems to justify – and he subscribes liberally to every patriotic fund. I believe he would be prepared to stand in his shop door and sing 'The absentminded beggar' [a Boer War song] all day. But his shop is a desert and picnics and jaunterings know him no more.[15]

Shand here lightly referred to a growing spirit of intolerance towards dissident opinion in Queensland which the anti-war *Worker* was colourfully reporting upon in the early months of 1900 under such headlines as 'Mob Rule' the 'Reign of Terror' and 'the Jingo Jamboree'.[16] In Stanthorpe, a man was assaulted for failing to stand at a toast to the Queen and in Rockhampton, the business premises of a Quaker pacifist were stoned and looted by a mob singing 'Sons of the Sea' and 'Soldiers of the

Queen' after the local press (Charles Buzacott's *Rockhampton bulletin*) called for his 'tar and feathering'.[17] Other manifestations of antagonism were reported from such disparate centres as Cairns, Charleville, Claremont, Mt Morgan, St George and Warwick.[18] In Brisbane, the *Worker* noted:

7.1 The crowd watching the result board at the Courier Building on Saturday night, 2 Sep. 1899 (JOL)

> The howling rabble ... have been rushing about looking for people who dared to think in opposition to the daily jingo press ... . Freedom of speech ... is suspended ... . Citizens are being assailed by larrikin barrackers, egged on and encouraged by the braggart press and the boycott against [dissident] business people ... is covertly commended and applied ... 'the sack' is also threatened and acted upon and the consequence is that timid opponents are cowed into silence and submission.[19]

On 10 February the paper reported that half a dozen foreign, largely German, sounding names had been removed from the Justice of the Peace list, and four nights later another violent clash occurred at Centennial Hall, when anti-war interjectors attempted to disrupt a loyalist meeting and were roughly ejected. Soon after, the home of an outspoken 'pro-Boer', Wallace Nelson, was attacked and his windows broken by a pack of stone-throwing jingoes. It was not until April 1900 that the *Worker* reported that 'mob law' was 'showing signs of drawing a to a close'.[20]

Several months later in October, however, there was another dramatic display of public stone-throwing in Brisbane. Though Lawson's study argues that 'religious sectarianism' was no threat to the prevailing social order, it was in reality the cause of the most tumultuous and serious rioting of the period.

On this occasion the venue was the Protestant Hall, Ann Street, and the assailants were several thousand enraged Irish roman catholics. The provocation was the visit of an ex-catholic priest, Joseph Slattery – now an ordained baptist minister from Massachusetts – and his wife, (billed as an 'escaped nun') who had arrived to give a series of lectures on 'Why I left the Roman Catholic Priesthood', 'Secrets of the Confessional' and 'Convent Life'. Once again, the crowds went wild. The meetings were called under the auspices of the Loyal Orange Lodge and Slattery came with recommendations from 'some of the leading Orangemen and clergy of the world'.

On 29 October 1900 there were around 800 protestant ladies and gentlemen in the hall and some 1500 angry catholics milling about outside, thus setting the scene for a three-hour riot which the *Courier* alleged would 'live long in the memory of those who attended'.

As soon as Slattery rose to speak, disturbances broke out in the hall and one man rushed the stage to assault him, only to be violently ejected. Other catholics in the hall attempted to dislodge chairs bolted to the floor to hurl as weapons. But the principle danger came from a fusillade of large rocks 'half-bricks, sharp slate and stones several pound in weight' which began to rain down on the roof and crash through the hall's many windows.

With Slattery shouting that 'tools of the Roman priests' were attacking them, stone-throwing also commenced within the Hall itself – a woman's face was seriously cut and the two press reporters felled – and the audience panicked.

The *Brisbane courier* wrote:

> For a time, the din of the stones was terrific; the rattle on the roof was like a hail of bullets from a rifle regiment ... stones through the broken windows ... struck ladies on the face.
>
> The ladies were hurried into the side passages which having no windows gave a safe refuge though several of them were injured before they could reach there. The rest of the audience clustered along the walls.

As Slattery left the platform, an organised rush was made against him, which resulted in more fighting. The hail of stones and street-metal continued for half an hour.

Outside, the stone-throwing crowd had grown to 'thousands' while forty police, none of them mounted, attempted vainly to control them. Making wild rushes into the mob, they drove portions of the crowd down across Adelaide and into Queen Street. Those who remained, however, began physically to attack the harassed protestants as they left the darkened hall. Numerous people at this point were hit by rocks or attacked with sticks. Reporters and police were among the casualties. Several people had their clothing virtually torn off as several dozen rioters made organised assaults on the front and side doors of the hall in order to get at Slattery. Although no exact enumeration was attempted, it appears as though scores were injured, the hall was wrecked and many police were hurt.

Adopting a similar tone to the comments made a year earlier after Barton's visit, the *Brisbane courier* editorialised that Brisbane had been:

> ...disgraced by an organised and abominable attack upon a visitor claiming his right of free speech ... . It brands those ... responsible ... as savages and places the whole community on ... trial.
>
> If meetings cannot be held in Brisbane except such as the mob may approve then mob rule represents the weak link in our chain and we are no stronger than the mob, or those who may inspire or direct [them].

Slattery 'carried strife with him wherever he has gone', the paper admitted, but the Brisbane riot, '... was the worst scene which the lecturer had encountered in all his Australian experiences with the exception perhaps ... of Kalgoorlie where the trouble was attributed to the generally rough character of the inhabitants and the small force of police available'.

The *Worker* identified a more 'deep laid' class basis to the religious-rioting; while the local tailoring firm of Ebenston & Marr took advantage of the incident to run the advertisement:

Riot! Riot! Riot!
There is nothing like a Good Riot
to stir up public sentiment and
nothing like Cheap Prices and Good
Value to attract public sympathy.
HOW SHOULD THE PUBLIC COTTON TO THIS?
Light Summer Suits: £3/3/-
The Leading Tailors Amongst the Fashionable Classes.

The following evening Slattery appeared again at the now windowless, dilapidated Protestant Hall. 600-700 adventurous souls gathered to hear him and 2-3000 protesters and onlookers crowded Ann Street. But on this second occasion the mounted and foot police presence of 100, divided into four companies, was so strong that most of the violence was scotched. Rope barriers and police cordons held the crowd back. Stones were still thrown at the hall or shot from catapults and several arrests made, but as the audience dispersed and the street crowd attempted to close in on them, the twelve mounted police drove them back towards Wickam Terrace and Wharf Street.

Overall the *Courier* concluded:

> It was quite by accident that several people were not killed ... it stands clear as noonday that Christianity and Civilization count for little when the white savage is roused and that liberty of speech is nothing where the mob is concerned.[21]

The final two episodes were less spectacular than the above mentioned riots, but they also demonstrate substantial conflict, a severe abrogation of civil rights – and one of them did result in a serious loss of life.

A little more than six months after the Slatterys' arrival, the metropolis was agog with the visit of another foreign couple – the Duke and Duchess of Cornwall and York. In George Street, the Southern Aboriginal protector, Archibald Meston arranged the construction of a massive Aboriginal arch, covered with tea-tree bark and decorated with grass-trees, staghorns and ferns. On its buttresses sat Aboriginal women and children with animal skins, dilly bags, mats and weapons displayed before them; and around the outer circumference of the arch stood weapon-carrying Aboriginal warriors many of them six feet in height, their bodies daubed with red and white ochre.

As the royal party passed beneath on 21 May 1901 Aboriginal women began to sing a traditional song of war, the men then joining in.[22] Sir Donald MacKenzie Wallace, Assistant Private Secretary to the royal couple, had this to say in his diary: 'Of the fauna ... we notice one genus which was conspicuous by its absence in Melbourne – the aboriginal population ... on this occasion ... used for decorative purposes, having a triumphal arch all to themselves'.[23]

7.2 The royal party passing beneath the Aboriginal arch, George Street, May 1901 (JOL)

The following evening at Government House at Gardens Point (or MI-AN-JIN as the Turrbul people had traditionally called it), Meston attempted to repeat his triumph by gathering the seventy-two Aborigines concerned for a corroboree to be performed after dinner for the royal party in the Government House grounds. Wallace described the event:

> As soon as their Royal Highnesses appear on the verandah... a group of aboriginals in their warpaint rush out into the open, brandishing their weapons and gesticulating violently while their women, concealed in the bushes chant in monotonous tones and beat time with their hands.

7.3 The royal party at the Domain, May 1901 (JOL)

The significance of it all was somewhat lost on the royal party. Wallace described it as 'unintelligible dumb-crambo pantomime': '...as we are totally unacquainted with the tribal traditions in question, [he confessed] we cannot grasp much of the inner meaning ... '. But as the night was 'somewhat chilly' and the performers were 'no longer accustomed to the scanty garb of their uncivilized forefathers', Wallace continued:

> ... proceedings are curtailed and refreshments are handed around by the Governor's servants .... For the first time perhaps in Australian history, half-naked savages ... are served by smart powdered footmen before Royalty. Not a bad subject for the satirists to write about 'Antipodean topsy-turvydom'. [24]

As the Aborigines ate, the Duke quizzed Meston on the possibility of saving the Aborigines from annihilation, but was told that they were unfortunately doomed.[25] What the official account did not include, however, was that the royal party had lingered rather too long over their meal that evening, and that the seventy-two Aborigines, to quote Meston's later angry words, 'were kept shivering and naked on a cold night with a heavy dew falling for an hour and a half after the time appointed for the performance ...' .[26]

Virtually all of these hand-picked 'fine specimens of humanity' caught influenza and bronchitis as a result of their exposure, and by September 1902 three of the men, Bismarck, Agnew and an unidentified male, had died from pneumonia.[27]

But Meston too had some blood on his hands. While the Aborigines were performing for royalty, forced Aboriginal removals to Fraser Island and Barambah reserves were proceeding apace. When the Keppel Islanders were removed in 1902, Oscar Morris wrote: 'they waved and cried and screamed never to see homeland again'.

And on Fraser Island, due to intense neglect, Meston's removals were dropping like flies from ankylostomiasis, or earth-eating disease. The alarmed anglican missionaries, who now ran the mission, could not control the outbreak and eventually loaded most of the survivors forcibly upon a ship, the *Rio Logue* and took them to Yarrabah in North Queensland.[28]

While the *Rio Logue* sailed northward, the movements of another vessel, the *Kumano Maru* heading south in January 1902, began to assume importance. As well as the English passengers on board this luxurious vessel were fifty Japanese who, despite the recent introduction of the Immigration Restriction Act, would be permitted to land in Australia as they carried pre-existing labour agreements. Also on the ship, however, were two Indian Hindus, who had boarded in Hong Kong, en route to Townsville. They were British subjects and ex-Indian Army members. They had never heard of the White Australia Policy.

At Townsville they became the first of many thousands to follow who would be given the bogus dictation test to deny them entry. When they predictably failed the test, they attempted to land anyway but were prevented by customs officials on the wharf and forced back on board. At Brisbane, on Pinkenba Wharf, the two tried again to escape the ship. Both ran down the gangway, but as the Hindus made their way across the wharf, an alarm was raised and a group of the Japanese passengers pursued and captured them. The *Brisbane courier* noted their further resistance:

> They, however, would not return to the ship and force had to be used to get them on board again. One of the men had to be roped and dragged on deck, but the other after a vain scuffle was more easily taken ... where they were handcuffed and eventually secured in the lazarette.

Alex Marks, the Japanese Consul, who happened to be on board the *Kumano Maru* and witnessed the unedifying spectacle, spoke to reporters of the great alarm the new immigration law was causing in Asia, especially Japan. A South African passenger protested against the treatment of the British Army officers but to no avail. The White Australia Policy had arrived.[29]

The fact that the two troublesome Hindus had been placed in the Peel Island leper lazarette was symbolically significant. Leprosy and racial reclusion were closely aligned and the Queensland Labor

Party had exploited a coloured leper scare on its way to becoming the first Labor Government in the world in December 1899.[30]

In 1900-01 as bubonic plague broke out in Brisbane, Asians and Melanesians again were freighted with the blame. The *Worker* of May 1900 commented that non-whites were 'peculiarly susceptible to dirt diseases':

> The dreadful bubonic plague first broke out in Asia and ... carried by Asiatic people and Asiatic merchandise ... at length ... has reached Australia. Already the Asiatic has implanted amongst us the loathsome disease of leprosy ... . But should the bubonic plague ... find its way amongst the Aborigines, Kanakas, Chinese, Japs and Hindoos who are in Queensland we may well cry 'May the lord have mercy on us'.[31]

So what can be made of these fractious episodes – the federation riot, the Boer War clashes, the sectarian disturbances as well as the Doomed Race and White Australia tableaux at Gardens Point and Pinkenba – all occurring in Brisbane between September 1899 and January 1902, supposedly an especially quiet period on the Quiet Continent?

To begin with, the incidents add substance to an historiography which indicates social conflict and contradictory cultural impulses rather than one which single-mindedly emphasises quiescence and consensus. We need to treat with caution assertions about Brisbane's lack of historical passion, its soullessness and its law-abiding nature.

It is also significant to note that each disturbance like the prior anti-Chinese riots, the subsequent 1912 strike and the conscription and Red Flag riots involved fundamental denials of rights – freedom of speech and assembly and, in the race examples, the full gamut of civil and human rights – as well as displaying a rampant sense of intolerance.

Boer War disturbances occurred in other parts of Australia – as they did, dramatically, in Great Britain, but the federation and sectarian rioting in Brisbane was virtually the worst in Australia. The treatment of the Aborigines and the Hindus resonated with intimations of Queensland's frontline frontier experiences. This was not a place where human freedoms outside of the Anglo-protestant, loyalist fold were very highly regarded.

Another salient feature of the riots and disturbances was the usually inept performance of the police. Similar claims could be made about the 1888 and 1919 riots as well as the 1912 General Strike. The police force seemed to fluctuate between being spectacularly under-prepared and caught unawares, and displaying massive over-reaction. The technique of appropriate, pro-active crowd control seemed to be somewhat beyond them.

In 1919 the Acting Prime Minister, W.A. Watt, laconically remarked in federal parliament: 'Strange things occur in Brisbane now and then' – and the other federal MPs seemed to know exactly what he was talking about.[32]

Brisbane, 'poor shabby, unromantic Brisbane' as David Malouf called it, beckons us still as an historical paradox – at once 'a place where nothing happened' as Johnno scoffed; and a place where anything at any moment might happen ... . Perhaps.

Timeline

1847 Earl Grey, Secretary of State for the colonies, proposed a general assembly for Australia to deal with tariffs, postal services, intercolonial roads and railways.

1849 Australian Colonies Government Act separated Victoria from NSW and provided for legislative councils in South Australia and Van Diemens Land.

1853 Committee of the NSW Legislative Council, chaired by William Wentworth, proposed a general assembly for the colonies.

1857 William Wentworth in London prepared a memorial for the secretary of state for the colonies, arguing for a federal assembly.

1859 Moreton Bay District separated from NSW, as Queensland.

1867 Intercolonial Postal Conference in Melbourne resolved there should be a federal council.

1868 British government refused to pass NSW Bill for the federal council.

1870 Victorian Royal Commission on Federation.

1871 Australian Natives Association formed in Melbourne.

1873 Australian Colonies Duties Act passed by the British Parliament, allowing the colonies to levy differential tariffs against each other.

1875 Rev. Dr J.D. Lang addressed Australian Natives Association in Brisbane on federation.

1881 Intercolonial conference in Sydney resolved there should be a federal council.

1883 Queensland Premier Thomas McIlwraith claimed New Guinea for the British crown to keep out Germany; Britain disallowed the annexation.
Intercolonial conference at Sydney supported establishment of a Federal Council; Griffith drafted a constitution.
Discussions held at conference on annexations, cost of cable and communication, and the expanding interests of France in the Pacific; agreement to meet every two years.
T.J. Byrnes, later premier, occupied Petrie Terrace dwellings.

1884 Queensland Parliament resolved to constitute Federal Council of Australasia on motion of Samuel Griffith.

1885 Federal Council of Australasia Act passed by British parliament.
Australian Natives Association branch re-established in Brisbane.
Queensland government steam yacht 'Lucinda' arrived at Brisbane.

1888 Federated republic envisaged by William Lane in his *Boomerang* editorial.
Holy Cross Laundry and Magdalen Asylum for women opened at Wooloowin.

1889 Major-General James Edwards reported on defence capabilities of the colonies.
Henry Parkes discussed federation with politicians at the Queensland Club and Belle Vue Hotel.
Parkes delivered his Tenterfield oration in favour of federation.

1890 Australasian Federation Conference, including Griffith and John Macrossan from Queensland, discussed Parkes' federation proposals in Melbourne (14 February).
Federation meeting at Exhibition Grounds (8 April).
Griffith elected premier in coalition with McIlwraith (August).
Australian Republican Association formed in Brisbane (September).
Australian Natives Association Conference on Federation.
Increasing signs of economic depression signified end of the boom era in Australia and start of the 'Federation era'.

1891 Federal Council opened at Hobart (20 January).
National Australasian Federation Convention in Sydney, with Parkes as president and Griffith as vice-president, agreed to adopt the name Commonwealth of Australia and draft a constitution; Queensland represented by John Donaldson, Samuel Griffith, John Macrossan, Thomas Macdonald-Paterson, Thomas McIlwraith, Arthur Rutledge and Andrew Thynne (March).
Griffith and others revised draft of the Commonwealth Constitution on Queensland government steamer 'Lucinda' at Hawkesbury River (to 29 March).
Macrossan died during convention (30 March) and interred at Nudgee Cemetery (3 April).
Federation Convention adopted draft constitution (9 April).
Negotiations for submitting federation proposals to the people failed (19 May).
Stylish new Exhibition Building built at Bowen Park.

1892 Constitution Bill introduced into Queensland parliament (23 June).

1893 Sir Samuel Griffith appointed chief justice of Queensland (13 March).
Hugh Nelson elected premier of Queensland (27 March).
Australasian Federation League formed in NSW (22 June).
Peoples Convention at Corowa (31 July) passed plan for a new constitutional process endorsed by popular vote.

1894 Brisbane Trades Hall opened in Turbot Street.
First annual meeting of Womans Equal Franchise Association at Trades Hall re-elected Emma Miller as president.

1895 Premiers Conference at Hobart, attended by Premier Hugh Nelson, adopted the Corowa plan (29 January).
Enabling Acts for a new convention passed in SA and NSW.
Queensland National Art Gallery opened in Town Hall building, Queen Street.
Stylish Smellie & Co. warehouse built in industrial precinct, Edward Street.

1896 Enabling Bill introduced in Queensland parliament but not passed (18 June).
Enabling Acts passed in Tasmania, Victoria and Western Australia.
Death of Sir Henry Parkes.
Enabling Act passed by Queensland parliament (4 November).
Bathurst Peoples Federal Convention (17 November).

1897 Election of convention delegates in Victoria, Tasmania, NSW and SA by popular vote.
Western Australian parliament elected its delegates.
First session of Australasian Federal Convention in Adelaide, except Queensland (22 March).
Draft Constitution Bill accepted by Convention (22 April).
Queen Victoria's Diamond Jubilee Day celebrations (21 June).
Aboriginals Protection Act passed.
Aboriginal Girls Home established at Hill End.
Second session of the Australasian Federal Convention in Sydney (2 September).

1898 Third session of Federal Convention at Melbourne (20 January).
Convention adopted draft constitution of the Australian Commonwealth.
Referendums on the Constitution Bill in NSW (unsuccessful), Victoria, Tasmania and SA.
Thomas J. Byrnes elected premier of Queensland (13 April), but died (27 September).
James Dickson elected premier of Queensland (1 October).
First Womens Federal League formed in Sydney.
Federation Leagues formed in Queensland, Tasmania and Western Australia.

1899 Secret Premiers Conference in Melbourne agreed to amend the Constitution Bill for NSW and Queensland, represented for first time since 1895 by Premier Dickson (29 January).
James Drake ran federation paper *Progress* (to Jan 1901).
Federation meeting at Corinda School of Arts (2 February).
Federation meeting at South Brisbane Technical College (1 March).
Queensland Anti-Convention Bill League opened its campaign (28 April).
Successful referendums held in SA, NSW, Tasmania and Victoria (April, June and July).

Anti-Billite meeting at the Alliance Hall, Woolloongabba (11 May).
Barton and Deakin addressed monster meeting of Queensland Federation League at the Exhibition Hall (12 May).
Griffith spoke on Australian Federation and the Constitution Bill at Brisbane School of Arts (26 May).
Federation meeting at Kelvin Grove School (May).
Federation meeting at Exhibition Building (7 August).
Anti-Billite meeting at Foresters Hall, Paddington (24 August).
Anti-Billite meeting at Kangaroo Point School of Arts (25 August).
Federation meeting at Leichhardt Street School, Spring Hill (25 August).
Federation meeting at Knowsley Hall, Stones Corner (25 August).
Federation meeting at Milton School (25 August).
Anti-Billite meeting on vacant corner at South Brisbane Railway Station (26 August).
Federation meeting on corner opposite Montague Hotel, South Brisbane (28 August).
Federation meeting at Highgate Hill reservoir, Gladstone Road (28 August).
Anti-Billite meeting at Corinda School of Arts (28 August).
Dr Carty Salmon of Victoria addressed Australian Natives Association on federation at Brisbane School of Arts (29 August).
Federation meeting at Corinda School of Arts (29 August).
Anti-Billite meeting at the Alliance Hall, Woolloongabba (29 August).
Federation meeting for officials at the Customs House (30 August).
Federation meeting at Foresters Hall, Fortitude Valley (30 August).
Anti-Billite meeting at Knowsley Hall, Coorparoo (30 August).
Federation meeting at Fiveways Hall, Woolloongabba (30 August).
Federation meeting at South Brisbane Technical College (30 August).
Federation meeting at Alliance Hall, Woolloongabba (31 August).
Federation meeting at Botanic Gardens gates (1 September).
Monster federation rally at Centennial Hall addressed by Barton and others (1 September).
Final demonstration by Anti-Billites at Town Hall reserve (1 September).
Queensland referendum accepted Constitution Bill despite Brisbane minority (2 September).
Federalists including Barton, Dickson and Thynne celebrated at the Imperial Hotel and addressed crowds from the Courier Building's balcony (2 September).
Queensland parliament voted to send an address to the Queen to establish the Commonwealth (4 October).
Boer War began in South Africa (5 October).
First Queensland contingent left from Pinkenba for South Africa (1 Nov).
Anderson Dawson elected premier of the first Labour government in the world (1 December).
Federalist Robert Philp elected premier (7 December).

1900 Former premier Sir Thomas McIlwraith died in London.
New bandstand replaced the old one in Botanic Gardens.
First federal Labour platform drawn up (24 January).
Patriotic carnivals on the Brisbane River and at the Botanic Gardens (10-11 March).
First case of bubonic plague at Woolloongabba (27 April).
Delegation to London including Dickson witnessed passage of Commonwealth of Australia Act through imperial parliament (5 July).
Commonwealth Act received royal assent (9 July).
Announcement that Lord Hopetoun was to be first governor-general (14 July).
Successful referendum in Western Australia (31 July).
Proclamation of the Commonwealth of Australia by Queen Victoria (17 September).
Governor-General Lord Hopetoun appointed William Lyne as first prime minister.
Edmund Barton commissioned to form the first federal ministry instead (24 December).
George Essex Evans won Australian poetry competition with his 'Federal ode' (31 December).
Special Commonwealth service of Presbyterian Church at St Pauls, Spring Hill (31 December).

End of the 'Colonial era' in Australia.

1901 Commonwealth of Australia proclaimed and Executive Council sworn in at Sydney; Premier Philp attended the celebrations.
Commonwealth Day festivities in Brisbane (1 January).
Special services in honour of Federation at Albert Street Wesleyan Church (1 January).
Federation ceremony at Fortitude Valley School including Evans' Ode (1 January).
New Queensland Museum building opened in former Exhibition Hall (1 January).
Death of Sir James Dickson, Minister for Defence, in Sydney (10 January), interred at Nundah (12 January).
Stylish Naval Offices building erected in Edward Street.
Death of Queen Victoria marked end of the 'Victorian era' (22 January).
Memorial service to honour the queen at St Johns Pro-Cathedral (27 January).
First federal flag for sale at T.C. Beirne's store in Fortitude Valley (27 January).
Proclamation of Edward VII's accession read by Governor Lord Lamington at Government House (1 February).
Day of mourning for Queen Victoria (2 February).
Customs, Defence, Postal and Telegraph departments taken over by the Commonwealth (1 March).
Prime Minister Barton addressed large meeting at Exhibition Building (2 March).
March of imperial troops in Brisbane celebrating Empire and Commonwealth (17 March).
First federal elections won by Protectionists and Barton elected prime minister (29-30 March).
Thomas Macdonald-Paterson elected federal member for Brisbane.
James Drake elected to the Senate and became postmaster-general.
Opening of first Commonwealth Parliament in Melbourne by Duke of Cornwall & York (9 May).
Ceremony of the hoisting of the Union Jack performed in Queensland schools (14 May).
Central Railway Station opened.
Arrival of Duke and Duchess of Cornwall & York by train (20 May).
Procession by Duke and Duchess drew vast crowds (21 May).
Children's choral performance in the Domain (22 May).
Duke reviewed Queensland Defence Forces returned from the South African War at Fort Lytton (21 May).
Duke laid foundation stone of St Johns Cathedral (22 May).
Duke and Duchess held reception at Government House (23 May).
Civic concert in honour of Duke & Duchess at Exhibition Grounds (23 May).
Duke & Duchess left Brisbane from Central Railway Station (24 May).
Griffith sworn in as lieutenant-governor of Queensland (21 June).
Dr Zillman spoke on commonwealth dangers at Brisbane School of Arts (1 July).
First federal budget delivered (8 October).
Queensland protest against federal legislation on Pacific Island labour (21 October).
Commonwealth government passed Immigration Restriction Act to end Pacific Island labour (17 December).
Land Administration Building begun in George and William streets (to 1905).
Federalist Arthur Rutledge occupied Lutwyche Chambers in Adelaide Street.

1902 First Commonwealth contingent from Queensland departed for South African War from Pinkenba (26 January).
Foundation stone of Morningside Methodist Church laid (2 February).
Demonstrations at the Exhibition Grounds in support of South African War (18 February).
Queensland Public Library opened in William Street (29 April).
Commonwealth Public Service Act passed (5 May); first department was Trade & Customs.
South African war memorial for Lachlan Caskey unveiled at Toowong Cemetery.
White Australian women gained right to vote in federal elections.
Statue of late T.J. Byrnes unveiled at Petrie Bight (22 August).

1903 South African war memorial for John Anning unveiled at Hemmant.
Sir Samuel Griffith retired as chief justice of Queensland and lieutenant-governor of Queensland to become chief justice of the new High Court of Australia (9 October).
First sitting of the High Court in Queensland at Supreme Court building (26 October).

1904 Recruitment of Pacific Islanders ceased in Australia.
Commonwealth Defence Act of 1903 came into effect (1 March).
Queensland's William Creswell of Borva House appointed commonwealth naval commandant.

1905 White Australian women gained right to vote in Queensland state elections.
Stylish Woolloongabba Post Office building opened.
Davies' 'Green House' built in Federation Queen-Anne style on Wickham Terrace.

1906 Commonwealth gained control of territory of Papua from Britain and Queensland.
Curators Cottage built in Federation Queen-Anne style in Botanic Gardens.
Statue of Queen Victoria unveiled in Queens Gardens.

1908 First official Australian coat of arms designed.

1909 Activist Emma Miller moved to family house at Red Hill.

1915 First World War signified end of the Federation era in Australia.

Measures

See manuals for more exact conversion tables, especially for larger multiples.

Area	
perch (p): 30.25 square yards	25.3 square metres (m^2)
rood (rd): 40 perches	1012 square metres
acre (ac): 4 roods	0.405 hectare (ha)
square mile: 640 acres	259 hectares
Distance	
inch (")	25.4 millimetres (mm)
foot ('): 12 inches (ins)	30.5 centimetres (cm)
yard: 3 feet (ft)	0.914 metres (m)
chain: 22 yards	20.1 metres
furlong: 10 chains	201 metres
mile (m): 1760 yards	1.61 kilometres (km)
fathom: 6 feet depth	1.83 metres
Liquid	
pint (pt)	568 millilitre (ml)
gallon (gal): 8 pints	4.55 litres (L)
Money	
penny (d)	4 farthings (1/4 d) or 2 halfpennies (1/2 d)
1d in 1890s	31c in 1920s-30s, 42c in 1999
shilling (/-)	12 pence
1/- in 1890s	$3.76 in 1920s-30s, $5 in 1999
pound (£)	20 shillings
£1 in 1890s	$75 in 1920s-30s, $100 in 1999
florin	2 shillings
sovereign	20 shillings
guinea (gn)	21 shillings
Temperature	
degrees (E)	32 fahrenheit = 0 celsius
C	(f - 32) x 5 ÷ 9
Weight	
ounce (oz)	28.3 grams (g)
pound (lb)	16 ounces = 0.454 kilograms (kg)
stone (st)	14 pounds = 6.35 kilograms
ton	1.02 tonnes (t)

Abbreviations

Note the following abbreviations in notes, references and captions

ABCQS	ABC of Queensland statistics
ADB	Australian Dictionary of Biography
B	Bulletin
BC	Brisbane Courier
BCC	Brisbane City Council
BCCom	Brisbane Chamber of Commerce
BCM	Brisbane Chamber of Manufacturers
B&DSMU	Bundaberg and District Sugar Manufacturers Union.
BHG	Brisbane History Group
BMC	Brisbane Municipal Council
CCR	Commonwealth Census Reports
CPB	Commonwealth Production Bulletins
CPD	Commonwealth Parliamentary Debates
EN	Evening News
FL	Fryer Library, University of Queensland
F&SR	Factories & Shops Reports, Queensland Government
ICE	Institution of Civil Engineers
IMC	Ipswich Municipal Council
JCU	James Cook University of North Queensland
JOL	John Oxley Library, State Library of Queensland, Brisbane
MBCC	Minutes of the Brisbane City Council
MBMC	Minutes of the Brisbane Municipal Council
MCC	Maryborough Chamber of Commerce
ML	Mitchell Library, Sydney
MS	Manuscript
NLA	National Library of Australia, Canberra
PA	Pughs Almanac
PERS	Personal communication
Q	Queenslander
QCCI	Queensland Chamber of Commerce and Industry
QCM	Queensland Chamber of Manufacturers
QEA	Queensland Electrical Association
QEF	Queensland Employers Federation
QGG	Queensland Government Gazette
QIE	Queensland Institute of Engineers
QIME	Queensland Institute of Mechanical Engineers
QPD	Queensland Parliamentary Debates
QPP	Queensland Parliamentary Papers
QSA	Queensland State Archives
QSS	Statistics of the State of Queensland
QVP	Queensland Votes & Proceedings, Legislative Assembly
RHSQ	Royal Historical Society of Queensland, Brisbane
SMH	Sydney Morning Herald
T	Telegraph; Queensland Telegraph
TS	Typescript
UQ	University of Queensland

Notes

Chapter 1: *Katherine McConnel*, Brisbane: The key to federation?

1 Alcazar Press 1900, 180.

2 Brisbane Metropolitan area returns 10,168 against and 6140 for the Commonwealth Bill. Queensland Government 1899, 1.1:417.

3 BC 4 Sep.1899.

4 It is important to note that anti-billites opposed the version of the Commonwealth Bill accepted at the 1897/98 Adelaide Federal Convention at which Queensland was not represented and not federation in general. Anti-feds opposed the abstract principle of federation.

5 North Queensland register 11 Sep. 1899.

6 BC 4 Sep.1899. A Federation League had been established in 1898, however it remained largely inactive until May 1899 launched off its campaign.

7 EN 7 Nov. 1896 cited in Barton 1897. G.B. Barton was a historian and brother to Edmund Barton, the prominent federationist and first prime minister of Australia.

8 The higher 'yes' vote at the second referendum vote in the other colonies corroborated this assertion. Jenkins 1971, ii.

9 *Progress* was a Brisbane paper established largely to assist the federal cause in Queensland and outlined the degree of influence of these two papers. The *Telegraph*'s power was largely confined to Brisbane whereas the *Courier* was a more 'national' newspaper with wider circulation and influence throughout Queensland. *Progress* 9 Sep.1899.

10 *Worker* 15 Jul. 1899.

11 Lang 1861, 286-90; Knight 1898, 349-52. The persistence of this antipathy is clearly identifiable in the Alcazar Press 1900 extract quoted above.

12 *Week* 4 Aug.1899.

13 Bennett 1978, 195.

14 *Week* 4 Aug. 1899.

15 *Week* 25 Aug. 1899.

16 *Week* 18 Aug. 1899.

17 *Week* 1 Sep. 1899.

18 Alcazar Press 1900, 155.

19 de Voss 1952, 100; Doran 1981, 385.

20 What was ironical in the battle between anti-billites and separationists was that the key arguments advanced by those against the Commonwealth Bill; opposition to a remote seat of government and reduced control over revenue, were the same complaints put forward for territorial separation; *Wide Bay and Burnett News* 2 Sep.1899.

21 North Queensland register 31 Jul.1899.

22 *Week* 11 Aug.1899.

23 T 2 Sep.1899.

24 T 2 Sep.1899; *North Queensland register* 31 Jul.1899; Doran 1981, 385.

25 In North Queensland it was claimed that under federation living costs would be 20-25% cheaper; Jenkins 1979, 163.

26 George Thorn had been Queensland's premier in the 1870s. He remained in parliament as one of its longest serving members; QPD Session 1899, 82:245.

27 T 2 Sep.1899.

28 The *Queenslander* remarked on the 2 Sep. that in the North and Centre 'the question there is now not so much "Shall we have a majority?" but " How big is our majority going to be?"' In the North every electorate supported federation, the 'yes' vote representing 84 percent. In the Centre the 'yes' vote was 64 percent; Doran 1981, 388; Bolton & Waterson 1999, 118.

29 Lawson 1973, 58.

30 *Week* 8 Sep.1899.

31 Lawson notes that at least 8 of the 22 men who helped establish the Anti-convention Bill League were manufacturers. Lawson 1973, 58.

32 Cited in Bennett 1978, 195.

33 *Week* 11 Aug.1899.

34 Cited in Lawson 1973, 58.

35 Q 26 Aug.1899.

36 BC 1 Sep.1899.

37 Cited in Jenkins 1979, 175.

38 *Week* 8 Aug.1899; *North Queensland register* 11 Sep. 1899; Q 9 Sep.1899; *Western champion* 5 Sep.1899.

39 In-letters Premier's Department, semi-personal, QSA PRE/A1.

40 BC 1 Sep.1899.

41 North Queensland register 31 Jul.1899.

42 *Worker* 9 Sep.1899.

43 *Week* 1 Sep. 1899.

44 Evans discusses this incident in ch.7.

45 BC 2 Sep.1899.

46 Jenkins 1979, 12-15.

47 Review of reviews 15 May 1899.

48 *Review of reviews* 15 Mar.1899.

49 BC 1 Sep.1899.

50 B 29 Jul. 1899.

51 Lawson 1973, 59.

52 B 12 Aug.1899.

53 Review of reviews 15 Sep.1899.

54 *Progress* 9 Sep.1899.

55 BC 4 Sep.1899.

56 T 2 Sep.1899.

57 *Western champion* 15 Aug.1899.

58 B 16 Sep.1899.

Chapter 2: *Joanne Scott*, Federation: The view from the Chief Secretary's Department

1 This chapter is based on material collected as part of the History of the Queensland Premier's Department project which is funded by the Queensland Department of Premier and Cabinet. See also, Cohen & Wiltshire 1995.

2 QPD 1884, 43:103.

3 QPD 1886, 49:1.

4 QPD 1886, 49:1-2.

5 QPD 1898, 79:471.

6 QPD 1898, 79:472.

7 Dutton to the Under Secretary, Colonial Secretary's Office, Perth, 12 Oct. 1899, QSA PRE/Z5.

8 Letter from Philp to A. McLean, 9 July 1900, QSA PRE/Z6.

9 Letter from Under Secretary Dutton to J. Gasking, 13 Jul. 1898, QSA PRE/G1.

10 Copy of letter from Hugh Nelson to Prime Minister of NSW, 30 Aug. 1894, QSA PRE/5.

11 Letter from Philp to W.J. Lyne, Sydney, 12 Nov. 1900, QSA PRE/Z6.

12 Public Service Board, Report on the Chief Secretary's Office, 30 Sep. 1901, QSA B/1746.

13 Confidential letter from Dutton to all Under Secretaries, 18 Sep. 1900, QSA PRE/Z6.

14 Murphy 1990, 244.

15 Letter from Philp to Edmund Barton, 3 Dec. 1901, QSA PRE/89.

16 Letter from Philp to Barton, 11 Jan. 1901, QSA PRE/G20.

17 QPD 1902, 89:260.

18 Lack 1966-67, 246.

19 Report of the Agent-General for Queensland for the year 1902, QPP 1903, 2:17.

20 QPD 1910, 106:1350.

Chapter 3: *John Laverty*, Queensland local government in the federation decade

1 Report of the Royal Commission on Local Government of 1896, QVP 1896, 2:525-62; Minutes of Evidence, 563-801; Draft Bill, 803-06.

2 Greenwood & Laverty 1959, 211.

3 QPD 1902, 90:966. The BMC passed resolutions in 1890 and 1894 that the mayor be elected from the aldermen by the ratepayers and pressed the government for an appropriate amendment to the Local Government Acts. MBMC, 4 Mar. 1890, 6:3, 365; 26 Apr. 1894, 7:5, 90.

4 These reforms were instituted by the Local Authorities Acts Amendment Act of 1920.

5 Report of the Local Government Commission of 1896, S. 14, 26, QVP 1896, 2:550.

6 When introducing the bill, the Home Secretary intimated that the urgency of the legislation was due to the outbreak of bubonic plague and pointed out that one weakness of the existing law was the lack of an executive head of what might be called a health department. QPD 34:223. The Metropolitan Joint Board for the Prevention of Epidemic Diseases was set up under the direction of the Commissioner of Public Health to deal with the plague crisis. QGG 1900, 73:821-4. See Greenwood & Laverty 1959, 231-36, 266, 321-22, 332-33, 350, 420-22 for details concerning the operation of the health acts.

7 See Greenwood & Laverty 1959, 245-47, 431-44.

8 The Victoria Bridge Act of 1897 and the Victoria Bridge Act Amendment Act of 1898 provided for the government to meet half the cost of the bridge and for the constitution of a joint local authority consisting of metropolitan local authorities to maintain the bridge and meet the interest and redemption payments on a loan covering the remaining half of the cost and other debts.

9 Greenwood & Laverty 1959, 241-42. See Griffith's speech on the second reading of the Divisional Boards Act of 1887, QPD 1887, 52:378-39.

10 Mayoral Report 1902-03, 8, MBCC 1902-03.

11 Mayoral Report for 1902-03, 11.

12 Mayoral Report for 1902-03, 11. See also Mayoral Report for 1903-04, MBCC 1903-04.

13 *Local Government* 1916-17, 113; 344. See also Minutes of the South Brisbane City Council 1906, 378 and BC 4 Sep. 1907, 4. For detailed discussion of local government endowments, see Greenwood & Laverty 1959, 240-45, 371-73.

14 For details of loans to local authorities, see Greenwood & Laverty 1959, 244-45; 373-77, 390-99.

15 Report of the Royal Commission, 24, QPP 2:553. See also 684-85, 687.

16 See Greenwood & Laverty 1959, 450.

17 BC 22 Nov. 1902, 4; T 5 Dec. 1902.

18 Minutes of South Brisbane City Council 1903, 410.

19 BC 14 Sept. 1903; 11 Aug. 1908; QPP 1905, 1:688; QPD 1910, 106:1420.

20 For a detailed discussion of the Greater Brisbane movement see Greenwood & Laverty 1959, ch. 10.

Chapter 4: David Cameron, 'Intelligent Progress' or 'Injurious Curse'? Manufacturing and the business of federation

1 Burnley 1980, 55-59; Goodall 1987, 18-19.

2 This process is described as the Decentralised Commodity Export Model, see Cameron 1999.

3 'Summary: Interchange – exports & imports, 1900-14', QSS, QPP 1931, 1:20-3k.

4 'Estimated gross value of production in various industries – Queensland 1911-30', in ABCQS 1929, 199; 1932, 234. These estimates are based upon metropolitan wholesale market prices as generally applied to primary produce, average mineral and metals prices on international markets, and for manufacturing an estimate of crude value added by the process of manufacture.

5 The period of the long drought is generally defined as 1898 to 1902. However, official government reports note that the drought did not break across most of the affected areas of the state until the second half of 1903. Report of the Registrar-General on agricultural and pastoral statistics for 1903, QPP 1904, 1:1057.

6 'Trade – imports & exports, various countries, Queensland, 1909', ABCQS 1910, 34.

7 'Summary: Interchange – exports & imports, 1900-13', QSS, QPP 1931, 1:20-3k.

8 'Summary: Interchange – exports & imports, 1900-13' & 'Production – industries, 1900-13', QSS, QPP 1931, 1:20-3k; 30-4k.

9 'Production – table IV, area of crown lands leased for pastoral purposes and amount of rent received, 1860-1913', QSS, QPP 1914, 1:4k.

10 J. Stodart, Annual Report of the Brisbane Chamber of Commerce [BCCom], 1911-12, 22-3, JOL.

11 Powell 1991, 80-1.

12 Premier Kidston to H. Amphlett, 2 Feb. 1907, QSA PRE/A245, 1362; 'Summary – imports, 1900-13', QSS, QPP 1931, 1:24-5k.

13 Lewis 1973, 130-32.

14 'Production – industries, 1900-1913', 'Crown lands – alienation, 1900-1913', QSS, QPP 1931, 1:30-4k.

15 Williams 1975, 92.

16 Cloher 1975, 107.

17 Burnley 1980, 63.

18 See Queensland mining section in Davies 1997, 54-84.

19 For a snapshot of social attitudes towards federation and primary source material see Evans, Saunders, Moore & Jamieson 1997.

20 Lewis 1973, 78; Fitzgerald 1986, 296-98.

21 For some analyses of federation and Queensland see Jenkins 1979; Green 1952; Clark 1960.

22 Coghlan 1969, 2370-380. NSW, Victoria, Tasmania and South Australia first voted in their respective referendums in Jun. 1898. New South Wales at first rejected federation, but voted again in Jun. 1899 in the affirmative. The question was put to Queensland voters on 2 Sep. 1899 and passed. Western Australia also delayed its response but the question was finally put and accepted in Jul. 1900.

23 Henderson 1992, 136.

24 Jenkins 1979, i-iv; Mullins 1980, 231.

25 QPD 1902, 89:659-66; Townsville Chamber of Commerce to Premier Philp, 18 Sep. 1902, QSA PRE/A135, 8531; Henderson 1992, 133-36.

26 'Queensland under Federation', BC 25 Mar. 1905, 10; 'Brisbane Chamber of Commerce', BC 29 Apr. 1905; 'Queensland Employers Federation', BC 12 Aug. 1905, 14.

27 Jenkins 1979, i-iv, 121-2; Harris 1984, 75.

28 Henderson 1992, 133-36.

29 Jenkins 1979, 156-65.

30 Jenkins 1979, iv; see McConnel ch. 1.

31 'The Federal Tariff', BC 17 Jan. 1900, 4.

32 'Brisbane Chamber of Commerce', BC 18 Jul. 1901.

33 Coghlan 1969, 2358. The Braddon Clause was named after Sir Edward Braddon, premier of Tasmania 1894-99, who proposed the commonwealth financing clause in Section 87 of the Constitution of the Commonwealth of Australia.

34 Pope 1986, 26/1:23. The first universal tariff was the Kingston Tariff of 1902 which was primarily an exercise in revenue raising that, nevertheless, existed with the intention of assisting in the protection of local industries. The first purely protective tariff was the Lyne Tariff of 1908, see Hall 1971, 75; Crowley 1973, 38-39, 156. Western Australia was only required to reduce its tariff collection by 20% per year over five years to 1906. The fiscal process of federation was divided into three separate financial periods. The first was to 1902 when the first commonwealth tariff was allowed and the states could no longer collect tariffs. For the first two years the commonwealth was expected to confine itself to collecting existing excises to finance the establishment of its administrative services. During the second stage from 1903-1910 the commonwealth began to collect more revenue through customs and excise and to redistribute not less than 75% of this to the states in the form of grants. This stage was called the 'book-keeping period'. From 1911, the third stage, the commonwealth was to decide how these financial relations would function.

35 'Chamber of Manufacturers' & 'Brisbane Chamber of Commerce', BC 17 Jan. 1900, 4.

36 G. Stupart, MCC Annual Report 1902-03 & 1904-05, JOL; QEF Annual General Meeting, 18 Sep. 1899 & 14 Sep. 1900; QEF Minutes of meetings, Film 0090 V1/C1, 1886-1914, JOL. The Federated Employers' Union of Queensland was formed in 1886 and changed its name to the Queensland Employers' Federation in 1904.

37 Jenkins 1979, 156-65.

38 BCM was formed in late 1899 by several members of the BCCom. The BCCom believed that a body representative of Brisbane's and Queensland's manufacturing interests should attend the inter-colonial conferences on the federal tariff rather than the Chamber of Commerce. Correspondence dated 2 Oct. 1900 on a BCM letterhead was discovered at QSA and proves conclusively that the BCM preceded the QCM, see Letter from BCM to Premier Dickson, 2 Oct. 1900, QSA PRE/A70, 10292. Further research of local press and BCCom reports revealed the date of the BCM's formation to be 30 Oct. 1899, see 'The Federal Tariff', BC 31 Oct. 1899, 6. & 'Quarterly Report', BCCom Annual Report Jan. 1900. The only secondary source found to mention the BCM is Lawson 1973, 53.

39 Hall 1971, 111-37. The first conference, held in Melbourne between 8-15 Nov. 1899, had delegates from NSW, Victoria, South Australia, Tasmania and Queensland. The Queenslanders present were J.C. Donaldson (Pres.), Hon. A. Gibson MLC, C.E. Hayes, G. Agnew, T. Morrow, J.K. Stewart, and H.H. Grenfell (Acting Sec.). The second conference was held in Adelaide between 22-26 May 1900. Again five colonies were represented with Agnew, Morrow, and Grenfell joined by new delegates S. Larard, Edward Armour, and John Kitchen. The final conference was convened in Sydney in Oct. 1900, with Western Australia represented for the first time, and a full complement of Queenslanders, comprising Donaldson, Armour, Grenfell, Morrow, Agnew, Gibson and Larard (Sec.), with new representatives R.W. Thurlow, A.A. Davey, and A.J. Raymond.

40 'The Federal Tariff – Chamber of Manufacturers Formed', BC 31 Oct. 1899, 6.

41 Lougheed 1969, 20.

42 Carter, BCCom Annual Report, 1899-1900, 27-36.

43 The B&DSMU was established to represent the interests of the sugar manufacturers in the district and did so until wound up in 1920. 'QEF Meeting 23 Jun. 1920', QEF, Film 0090, V2/C1, 1915-1928, JOL.

44 'The Federal Tariff', BC 31 Oct. 1899; 'Quarterly Report', BCCom Annual Report Jan. 1900.

45 The committee consisted of J.D. Campbell, Angus Gibson, C.E. Hayes, T. Morrow, R. Hart, J.H. Forrest, J.C. Donaldson, J.R. Stewart, A. Clarke, J.K. Cannon, H. Barton, C.E. Bernays and a Mr Walthall.

46 'The Federal Tariff', BC 31 Oct. 1899, 6.

47 'The Federal Tariff: Brisbane Chamber of Manufacturers', BC 1 Nov. 1899, 4.

48 Lawson, 1973, 53. The BCM's membership reached 109 within three months.

49 Hall 1971, 111-37.

50 'Free-Trade and Protection', editorial, BC 2 Nov. 1899, 4.

51 'Free-Trade and Protection', editorial, BC 2 Nov. 1899, 4; 'Federal Tariff', editorial, BC 4 Jan. 1900, 4.

52 Hall 1971, 117; 'The Federal Tariff - Conference of Chambers of Manufacturers', BC 13 Nov. 1899, 5; 'Conference of Chamber of Manufacturers', BC 23 May 1900, 5; 'Brisbane Chamber of Manufacturers', BC 19 Jun. 1900, 8.

53 'Chamber of Manufacturers', BC 4 Jan. 1900, 4.

54 Letter from Clive Bubb, General Manager of the QCCI, to the author, 22 Aug. 1996. The existence of the BCM was unknown to the QCCI, the successor to the BCM and QCM. Indeed the company shell adopted by the QCCI in 1994 is that of the QCM dating back to 1911. Unfortunately the early records of the BCM and QCM appear to have been lost. The majority of the information on these organisations was gathered from the extant records of the QEF, correspondence found in the QSA, contemporary press reports, secondary sources dealing with Queensland employer organisations, and correspondence between the author and Bubb.

55 BCCom/BCM to Premier Philp, 19 Aug. 1903, QSA PRE/A157, 6088.

56 BCM to Digby Denham, Minister for Agriculture and Public Works and Premier Morgan, 18 Jul. 1904, PRE/A180, 4576, QSA.

57 G.T. Clarke, Secretary of the Federal Council of Chambers of Manufacturers to Premier Morgan, 15 Nov. 1904, PRE/A189, 7275, QSA.

58 'Chamber of Manufacturers', BC 11 Jun. 1904, 14.

59 Emil Sachs, of E. Sachs & Co., was a member of the BCM Council from at least 1901. His company began trading on 6 Jan. 1897 and established a tinsmithing works in Fortitude Valley. The company celebrated its centenary in 1997, and is run by Sach's grandson H.P.J (Peter) Sachs, and great-grandsons P.M. (Peter) and Michael Sachs. E. Sachs & Co. is one of only a handful of family-owned companies that have continued to operate for over one hundred years in Queensland. Indeed, of the 9000 companies registered in Queensland in 1997, only 129 have existed for a century or more, these mostly being the larger banks, pastoral companies and legal firms. H.P.J. Sachs has authored an extraordinary five volume business and family history, which includes oral histories, extracts of minutes, company documents, and family letters (many translated from German) dating back to 1856. Sachs's research is especially notable for its behind the scenes detail on business practices and relationships in Brisbane, and shows how one manufacturing firm came to grips with the sweeping changes, economic and social, which have impacted upon Queensland in the twentieth century. See Sachs 1997a; Sachs 1997b, Sachs 1997c; Sachs 1997d

60 'Chamber of Manufacturers', BC 11 Jun. 1904, 14.

61 'QEF – AGM, 28 Nov. 1904', QEF 1900-14, Film 0090 V1/C1, Reel 1, 1886-1914. JOL.

62 QEF Minutes, 2 Sept. 1915, QEF 1914-28, Film 0090, V2/C1, 1915-28, JOL. Some of these organisations included: the Brisbane/Queensland Boot Manufacturers Association, Brick Manufacturers Supplies Association, Confectioners Association, Ice Producers Association, Iron Masters Association, Master Bakers Association, Master Coachbuilders and Wheelwrights Association, Master Masons Association, Master Picture Framers Association, Master Printers Association, the Tinsmiths Association.

63 J. Leahy, BCCom Annual Report, 1900-01, 27, JOL.

64 A.J. Carter, BCCom Annual Report, 1899-1900, 36, JOL. Carter was president from 1898-1902 with the exception of 1900 when John Leahy held the position.

65 Jenkins 1979, 162.

66 A. M. Hertzberg, BCCom Annual Report 1903-04, 11-13, JOL.

67 A. M. Hertzberg, BCCom Annual Report 1904-05, 9, JOL.

68 A. M. Hertzberg, BCCom Annual Report 1903-04, 13, JOL.

69 'Queensland Under Federation', Letter to the editor, BC 25 Mar. 1905, 10.

70 J. W. Thurlow, BCCom Annual Report 1908-09, 7-8; & A.M. Hertzberg, BCCom Annual Report 1909-10, 11, JOL.

71 Cameron, Queensland Economy, Manufacturing and the Political Economy.

72 A.M. Hertzberg, 'Presidents's Annual Report', BCCom Annual Report 1903-4, 11-12. & 1904-5, 9 JOL; 'F&SR', QPP 1903, 2:129; D. Denham, QPD 1907, 99:638; Fitzgerald 1986, 298; B.J. Costar 1973, viii-ix; Laverty 1970, 40-1.

73 'Summary: Interchange - Exports & Imports, 1890-1913' & 'Production - Industries, 1900-1910', QSS, QPP 1931, 1:20-3k & 30-4k.

74 'Summary: Interchange - Imports, 1900-1910', QSS, QPP 1931, 1:24-5k.

75 Information on statistical administration and practices in Queensland supplied by Noel Mallory, Queensland Statistician's Office, Brisbane, 13 May 1997, PERS; 'F&SR, 1900', QPP 1901, 2:1591-92; 'F&SR, 1901', QPP 1902, 1:841; 'F&SR 1907', QPP 1907, 2:.297; 'F&SR 1917-18', QPP 1917-18, 1:.1315; 'F&SR 1908', QPP 1909, 2:85; 'F&SR 1919', QPP 1920, 2:684; 'F&SR 1920', QPP 1920, 2:112.

76 'Summary - Manufactories', QSS, QPP 1931, 1:20k.

77 In 1906 commonwealth statistics show that 1304 factories employing four or more employees were operating in Queensland, while the *Statistics* show that 1993 factories of two or more employees were operating. Comparable figures are only available for 1906 with 1304 factories employing four or more hands and 1993 factories with two or more hands; in 1907 (1359 and 1725); and 1908 (1371 and 1479). Figures for the period 1906-1908 show a steep decline in the number of smaller factories, from 35% of all factories in 1906 to 7% by 1908. The ratio of small to large factories may have been much larger in 1900 than is demonstrable in 1906. Australian Bureau of Statistics, CPB 1911, Table 114, no. 6, 63. & CPB 1920, Table 129, no. 14, 87;.'Factory Tables' in F&SR 1900-11, QPP 1901, 2:1594; QPP 1902, 841; QPP 1903, 2:124; QPP 1904, 1, 708; QPP 1905, 1:642; QPP 1906, 1:1582; QPP 1907, 2:309; QPP 1908, 2:323; QPP 1909, 2:85; '1910', QPP 1910, 2:744; QPP 1911-12, 2:369; Table LXVII, QSS, QPP 1912, 2:56k; Table LXVIII, QSS, QPP 1913, 1:58k; Table LXIX, QSS, QPP 1914, 1:58k.

78 'Summary - Production', QSS, QPP 1931, 1:20k.

79 Barton 1909.

80 Barton 1909, 234-35, 239, 247, 251, 255, 259, 261, 263.

81 G. Stupart, MCC Annual Report 1902-03 & 1904-05, JOL.

82 For a more detailed analysis of this question see Barton 1909, ch. 3.

83 G. Stupart, MCC Annual Report 1902-03 & 1904-05, JOL.

84 Jenkins 1979, 156-64.

85 Queensland manufacturers were able to export, both interstate and overseas, items such as clothing, hats, timber furniture, doors and windows, saddlery and leatherware, beef, mutton, bacon, hams, cheese, butter, timber, refined metals. Lesina, QPD 1906, 97:233; Barton 1909, 232-38, 255-59; MCC Annual Report 1904-05, JOL.

86 Jenkins 1979, 156-64.

87 See, for example, the following historians who, to varying degrees, argue that federation adversely affected or retarded the development of the manufacturing sector in Queensland: Lougheed 1984, 27; Butlin 1970, 312; Laverty 1970, 40-41; Costar 1973, viii; Wiltshire 1980, 271; Fitzgerald 1986, 298.

88 See for example Stubbs-Brown 1962, 185, 189; Mullins 1980, 217; Jenkins 1979, 159-60; Lawson 1973, 59.

89 G. Stupart, MCC Annual Report 1902-03 & 1904-05, JOL; 'F&SR', QPP 1904, 1:726; J.W. Thurlow, BCCom Annual Report 1908-09, 7-8, JOL; Stubbs-Brown 1962, 185; Hughes 1980, 324.

Chapter 5: *Bill Oliver*, Brisbane engineers at federation – the men and their institutions

1 For the beginnings of civil engineers, see Lloyd 1991.

2 Highton 1852.

3 Buchanan, 56
4 Whitmore 1984; Cossins 1999.
5 McBride & Taylor 1997, 1.
6 QVP 1900, 1:49.
7 Rogan 1992, 19.
8 Watson & McKay 1994, 21.
9 Whitmore 1984, 13.
10 Davenport 1986, 366.
11 Whitmore 1984, 26-27.
12 PA 1902, 66.
13 QVP 1901, 1:513.
14 Leggett 1990.
15 George & Prentice 1989, 137.
16 Whitmore 1984, 27.
17 Whitmore 1984, 69.
18 QVP 1901, 1:108.
19 QVP 1901, 1:98.
20 Simmers 1992, 15.
21 Simmers 1992, 16.
22 Becconsall 1992, 7.
23 George 1990, 7.
24 Steer 1944.
25 Whitmore 1984, 9.
26 Barton 1901, 1.
27 Minutes of proceedings, IMC 7 Sep. 1896, QSA microfiche Z1333.
28 Cossins 1999, 48.
29 Corrie 1903, 26.
30 IMC 8 March 1897, QSA microfiche Z1333.
31 Whitmore 1984, 25.
32 PA 1902, 175.
33 Cossins 1999, 49
34 Hanlon 2000.
35 QVP 1901, 1:306.
36 QVP 1901, 1:214.
37 Steer 1944.
38 Steer 1944.
39 QVP 1901, 4:702.
40 Report to Directors for year ended 30 Dec. 1902, BETICI, JOL VF Serials 388 12.
41 Brisbane Gas Company Ltd 1954, New carbonising and ancillary plant 1954, JOL Q665.7.
42 Cossins 2000, 114-16.
43 Cossins 2000, 227.
44 Cossins 2000, 122.
45 Cossins 1999, 125.
46 Brisbane Board of Waterworks General Ledger No. 3, 30 Jun. 1902, BCC archives CAS 0275.
47 Cossins 1999 p 154
48 George & Prentice 1989,155.

49 QVP 1901, 1:275.

50 Watson & Mackay, 1994, 32.

51 Corrie 1903, 26.

Chapter 6: *John Mackenzie-Smith*. Two Queensland federation poets and the Red Page Razor

1 Palmer 1954, 1.

2 Stephens 1925, 76-80, 90-94.

3 A.G. Stephens 1901, back cover.

4 Evans, Saunders, Moore & Jamieson 1997, 199, 245.

5 Wilde 1994, 129-30.

6 A.G. Stephens 1901, Introductory (unpaginated).

7 Lindsay 1965, 38-39.

8 Rolfe 1979, 162.

9 Ibid, 161.

10 Stephens 1901, Introductory.

11 BC 11 Nov. 1909.

12 ADB, 7:195.

13 ADB, 8, 446.

14 Brunton Stephens to A.G. Stephens, 12 Nov. 1890 in Hadgraft 1969, 7.

15 Hadgraft 1969, 97.

16 SMH 19 July 1902.

17 Rolfe 1979, 164.

18 Hadgraft 1969, 57-60.

19 Ibid, 91.

20 Green 1966, 106-07.

21 BC 11 Nov. 1909.

22 Tardent 1901, 4.

23 Darling Downs gazette 11 Nov. 1909.

24 Wilde 1994, 260.

25 Evans 1928, 11.

26 BC 13 Nov. 1909.

27 Essex Evans Papers 1906, Biographical sketch by 'Bookworm', FL.

28 Evans 1928, 134.

29 Evans, 1928, 89.

30 *Spectator*, 8 Jan. 1910.

31 Evans 1928, 2-3.

32 Ackland, 1993, xix-xx.

33 Australasian critic, May 1891.

34 *Spectator*, 8 Jan. 1910.

35 Newspapaer cuttings, Essex Evans Papers, FL.

36 Ibid

37 Evans to Browne, 25 Apr. 1898, Poems and letters, JOL OM 66 027.

38 Ibid.

39 Palmer 1954, 110-11.

40 Kellow 1930, 162-63, 404.
41 Irving 1999a, 398-99, 431-32.
42 Irving 1999a, 34-36.
43 Stephens 1925, 1-2.
44 Ibid, 4-7.
45 Irving 1999a, 34-37, 40.
46 Stephens 1925, 12-13.
47 Evans 1928, 7-9, 227.
48 *Review of reviews* 15 Aug. 1900.
49 BC 2 Sep. 1899.
50 Ibid.
51 BC 4 Sep. 1899.
52 BC 1 Jan. 1901.
53 Stephens 1925, 11.
54 Tiffin 1991, 71.
55 Evans 1928, 4-6.
56 Holloway in Magery 1883, 151.
57 B 5 Jan. 1901.
58 B 19 Jan. 1901.
59 Evans to Deakin, 4 Oct. 1900, Deakin Collection, NLA MS 1540.
60 La Nauze 1965, 229.
61 Evans to Deakin, 14 Oct. 1900, Deakin Collection, NLA MS 1540.
62 Evans to Deakin, 12 May 1902, Deakin Collection, NLA MS 1540.
63 Evans to A.G. Stephens, 23 Mar. 1905, Essex Evans Papers NLA MS 79027.
64 Evans to A.G. Stephens, 19 Mar. 1901, Essex Evans Papers NLA MS 79027.
65 Evans to A.G. Stephens, 30 Mar. 1906, Essex Evans Papers NLA MS 79027
66 Evans to A.G. Stephens, 1 Jul. 1905, Essex Evans Papers NLA MS 79027.
67 Evans to A.G. Stephens, 30 Mar. 1906, Essex Evans Papers NLA MS 79027.
68 Evans 1928, 26.
69 South Wales daily news, 24 Sep. 1910.
70 BC 13 Nov. 1909.
71 Evans 1928, i.
72 Birchley 1978, 212.

Chapter 7: *Raymond Evans*, Brisbane at federation 1899 -1902

1 Malouf 1998, 116-17.
2 Lindsay 1985, 19, 369.
3 Evans 1986b, 5-15; Evans 1987, 100-12.
4 Lawson 1973, xvii, xxii, 29, 199-200, 316.
5 Lawson 1973, 81, 304, 316.
6 Lawson 1973, 23-24, 62-63, 184-85; Thorpe 1987, 19-29.
7 Stockwell 2000, 14, 19.
8 Wilson, 1971,13-20; Evans 1999, 79-94; Evans 1988; Evans 1985, 75-98; Evans 1986a, 10-17; Evans 1992, 126-171; Brockett 1993, 75-113; Thompson & Macklin 2001.
9 BHG 1985, 57-70; Evans 1988, 1-7.

10 Lindsay 1985, 67; Harman 1985, 86-93; Evans 1995, 1-26; Strahan 1984, 5-46; Stockwell 2000, 20.

11 Evans 1988, 5.

12 Hirst 2000, 225-35.

13 Birrell 2001, 127; Hirst 2000, 17, 23.

14 BC 3 Sep. 1899; *Progress* 2 & 9 Sep. 1899.

15 W. Shand, Brisbane, to Thomas Farrar, Surrey, 8 Apr. 1900, Farrar Family Papers, Surrey Records Office, Kingston-upon-Thames.

16 *Worker* 20 Jan., 10 Feb., 10 Mar. 1900.

17 *Worker* 10 & 31 Mar. 1900; Evans, Saunders, Moore & Jamieson 1997, 76-78.

18 *Worker* 3 & 17 Feb., 10 Mar., 23 May, 23 Jun. 1900; *Progress* 8 Mar., 23 May 1900.

19 *Worker* 27 Jan., 3 Feb. 1900.

20 *Worker* 10 Feb., 10 & 31 Mar. 1900.

21 BC 30 & 31 Oct.1900; *Worker* 10 Nov. 1900; *Worker* 10 Nov. 1900; Evans, Saunders, Moore & Jamieson 1997, 80-82.

22 Q 25 May 1901; BC 11 May 1901; A. Meston to Colonial Secretary, 25 Feb. 1901, QSA Col 144.

23 Wallace 1908, 45.

24 BC 22 May 1901; Wallace 1908, 46-48.

25 BC 23 May 1901; Wallace 1908, 46.

26 A. Meston, Southern Aboriginal Protector's report, 1 July 1901, QSA COL 143.

27 A. Meston, Report, 1 Jul., 23 Sep. 1901, QSA Col 144; BC 30 Jul. 1901.

28 O. Morris, Keppel Islands to Under Colonial Secretary, 11 Sep. 1902, QSA COL 144; Evans & Walker 1977, 89-91; Evans 1999, 111-13, 135-45.

29 BC 20 Jan. 1902; *Age* 21 Jan. 1902.

30 Evans, 'The politics of leprosy', forthcoming.

31 *Worker* 5 May 1900.

32 Evans 1988, 1.

33 Malouf 1998, xvii.

References

Alcazar Press 1900, comp. Queensland 1900: A narrative of her past together with biographies of her leading men, Brisbane.

Barton, G.B. 1897 Papers MS 79: Press Cuts 1897. ML NSW.

Bennett, Scott 1978 *Federation*, Cassell Australia, Melbourne.

Bolton, Geoffrey & Duncan Waterson 1999, 'Queensland', in ed. Helen Irving, *The centenary companion to Australian federation*, Cambridge University Press, Oakleigh.

Brisbane History Group 1986, *Brisbane at war*, ed. Helen Taylor, BHG papers no.4.

Brisbane History Group 1985, *Brisbane: Housing, health, the river and the arts*, ed Rod Fisher, BHG papers, no.3

Brisbane History Group 1991, *Brisbane: Mining, building, Story Bridge, the Windmill*, ed. Rod Fisher, BHG papers no.10.

Cohen, Kay & Kenneth Wiltshire 1995, *People, places and policies: Aspects of Queensland government administration 1859-1920*, UQPress, St Lucia.

de Voss, V.R. 1952, Separatist movements in Central Queensland in the nineteenth century, BAhons thesis SU.

Doran, Christine 1981, North Queensland separatism in the nineteenth century, PhD thesis, JCU.

Evans, Raymond, Saunders, Kay, Moore, Clive & Brian Jamieson, 1997, *1901 - Our future's past: documenting Australia's federation*, Macmillian, Sydney.

Greenwood Gordon & John Laverty 1959, *Brisbane 1859-1959: A history of local government*, BCC.

Jenkins, Alan 1979, Attitudes towards federation in Queensland, MA thesis. UQ.

Knight, John J. 1898, *In the early days: History and incident of pioneer Queensland,*. Sapsford, Brisbane.

Lack, Clem 1966-67, 'Some Queensland Agents-General: Horace Tozer and those who followed him', *Journal of the Royal Historical Society of Queensland*, 8/2: 246-85.

Lang, J.D. 1861, *Queensland Australia*, Edward Stanford, London.

Lawson, R.L. 1973, *Brisbane in the 1890s: A study of an Australian urban society*, UQPress, Brisbane.

McConnel, Katherine 1999, "Separation is from the Devil while Federation is from Heaven': The Separation Question and Federation in Queensland', *The New Federalist* 4:14-21.

Murphy, Denis J., Joyce, Roger B. & Colin A. Hughes, eds, 1980, *Labor in power: The Labor Party and government in Queensland 1915-57*, UQPress, Brisbane.

Murphy, Denis J., Joyce, Roger B. & Colin A Hughes. eds, 1970, *Prelude to power: The rise of the Labor Party in Queensland 1885-1915*, Jacaranda Press, Brisbane.

Murphy, Denis J., Joyce, Roger B. & M.Cribb, eds, *The premiers of Queensland*, rev. ed., UQPress, St Lucia.

Queensland Government 1899, *Journal of the Legislative Council of Queensland: 1899.* Edmund Gregory, Government Printer, Brisbane. 1.1:417.

Rhodes, Glen 1988, The Australian federation referenda 1898-1900: A spatial analysis of voting behaviour, PhD thesis, London School of Economics & Political Science, London.

Watson, Donald & Judith McKay 1994, *Queensland architects of the 19th century,* Queensland Museum, Brisbane.

Entrepreneurs and Engineers

Barton, E.C. 1901, *Inaugural address,* Queensland Institute of Engineers, H. Pole, Brisbane.

Barton, E.J.T. 1909, *Jubilee history of Queensland: A record of political, industrial, and social development*, H.J. Didamms & Co, Brisbane.

Becconsall, B.J. 1992, *Electric lighting in Brisbane – the first decade 1882-1892: Power supply*, Institution of Engineers, Australia (Queensland Division), Queensland Division Technical Papers 33/4.

Brisbane Board of Waterworks 1902, General Ledger no. 3, 30 June. J Hicks Ltd. BCC Archives CAS 0275.

Brisbane Chamber of Commerce 1900-18, *Brisbane Chamber of Commerce Annual Reports*, Brisbane Chamber of Commerce, Brisbane.

Brisbane Electric Tramways Investment Company Limited 1902, Report to Directors for the year ended 30 December 1902, JOL VF Serials 388.12

Brisbane Gas Company Ltd 1954, *New carbonising and ancillary plant 1954,* JOL Q665.7 new.

Burnley, Ian H. 1980, *The Australian urban system: Growth, change and differentiation*, Longman Cheshire, Melbourne.

Butlin, Noel G. 1970, 'Some perspectives of Australian economic development, 1890-1965', in C. Forster, ed., *Australian economic development in the twentieth century*, George Allen & Unwin, Sydney.

Cameron, David 1999, An historical assessment of economic development, manufacturing and the political economy in Queensland, 1900-30, Ph.D thesis, UQ.

Clark, K.N. 1960, An examination of Queensland attitudes to the federal system 1900-20, BAhons thesis, UQ.

Cloher, D.U. 1975, 'A perspective on Australian urbanisation', in Powell & Williams 1975.

Cochrane, Tom 1989, *Blockade: The Queensland Loans Affair 1920 to 1924*, UQ Press, Brisbane.

Coghlan, Timothy A. 1969, *Labour and industry in Australia: Volume IV*, Macmillan, Melbourne.

Commonwealth Bureau of Census & Statistics 1912, *Commonwealth of Australia, Production Bulletin No. 6.*

Commonwealth Bureau of Census & Statistics 1919, *Commonwealth of Australia, Production Bulletin No. 12.*

Corrie, Leslie G. 1903, *Minute of the Right Worshipful the Mayor for the mayoral year ended 4 February 1903,* Corporation of the City of Brisbane.

Cossins, Geoffrey 1966, *One hundred years of Brisban's water supply,* Institution of Engineers, Australia (Brisbane Division). Brisbane Division Technical Papers (pre-print) 7/10.

Cossins Geoffrey ed. 1999, *Eminent Queensland engineers volume 2,* Institution of Engineers, Australia, Queensland Division

Cossins, Geoffrey 2000, The Gold Creek story, TS, BCC libraries.

Costar, Brian J. 1973, Political and social aspects of the Great Depression in Queensland, 1929-1932, MA Qual. thesis, UQ.

Crowley, Frank K. ed. 1973, *Modern Australia in documents: Vol. 1, 1901-39*, Wren Publishing, Melbourne.

Davenport, W. ed. 1986, *Harbours & Marine: Port and harbour development in Queensland from 1824 to 1985*, Queensland Department of Harbours & Marine, Brisbane.

Davies, Mel 1997, *A bibliography of Australian mining history*, Australian Mining History Association, Perth.

Fitzgerald, Ross 1986, *A history of Queensland from the Dreaming to 1915*, UQPress, Brisbane.

French, Maurice 1989, *Conflict on the Condamine: Aborigines and the European invasion - A history of the Darling Downs frontier*, Darling Downs Institute Press, Toowoomba.

George, W.I. 1990, *Queensland Institute of Mechanical Engineers,* Institution of Engineers, Australia (Queensland Division), Queensland Division Technical Papers 31/20.

George, W.I. & S.A. Prentice 1989, *Some references to early professional engineering societies in Queensland (1890-1919).*

Hanlon, P. 2000, *'Oh-ver': History of the Brisbane Cross River Ferries*, The author.

Goodall, Brian 1987, *The Penguin dictionary of human geography*, Penguin, London.

Hall, C.R. 1971, *The manufacturers: Australian manufacturing achievements to 1960*, Angus & Robertson, Sydney.

Harris, C.P. 1984, *Regional economic development in Queensland 1859 to 1981 with particular emphasis on North Queensland*, ANU Centre for Research on Federal Financial Relations, Canberra.

Henderson, L. 1992, More than rates, roads and rubbish: A history of local government in action in Thuringowa Shire 1879-1985, James Cook University of North Queensland PhD thesis.

Highton, Edward 1852, *The electric telegraph: Its history and progress*, John Weale, London.

Hughes, Colin 1980a, *The government of Queensland*, UQPress, Brisbane.

Hughes, Colin 1980b, 'Land and settlement' in Murphy, Joyce & Hughes 1980.

Ipswich Municipal Council, Minutes of proceedings, QSA microfiche Z1333

Jenkins, Alan 1979, Attitudes towards federation in Queensland, MA thesis, UQ.

Johnston, W. Ross 1982, *The call of the land: A history of Queensland to the present day*, Jacaranda Press, Brisbane.

Laverty, John 1970, 'The Queensland economy 1860-1915' in Murphy, Joyce & Hughes 1970.

Lawson, R.L. 1973, *Brisbane in the 1890s: A study of an Australian urban society*, UQPress, Brisbane.

Leggett, B.C. 1990, List of signatories of early Brisbane City Engineer's Department drawings, BCC Archives.

Lewis, Glen 1973, *A history of the ports of Queensland: A study in economic nationalism*, UQPress, St. Lucia.

Lloyd, B.E. 1991, *Engineers in Australia: A profession in transition*, Macmillan, Melbourne.

Lougheed, Alan 1969, *A century of service: History of the Brisbane Chamber of Commerce 1868-1968*, Brisbane Chamber of Commerce, Brisbane.

Lougheed, Alan 1984, *The Brisbane Stock Exchange, 1884-1984*, Boolarong Publications, Brisbane.

Maryborough Chamber of Commerce 1905, *Maryborough Chamber of Commerce Annual Report 1904-05*, Maryborough Chamber of Commerce, Maryborough.

McBride, Frank & Helen Taylor 1997, *Brisbane 100 stories,* BCC.

Mullins, Pat 1980, 'Australian urbanisation and Queensland's underdevelopment: A first empirical statement', *International journal of urban and regional research*, 4:212-38.

Murphy, D.J. 1980, 'State Enterprises', in Murphy, Joyce & Hughes 1980.

Murphy, D.J. 1990, 'William Kidston: A tenacious reformer', in Murphy, Joyce & Cribb 1990, 221-61.

Murphy, D.J., Joyce, Roger B. & Colin A. Hughes eds, 1980, *Labor in power: The Labor Party and government in Queensland 1915-1957*, UQPress, Brisbane.

Murphy, D.J., Joyce, Roger B. & Colin A Hughes eds, 1970, *Prelude to power: The rise of the Labor Party in Queensland 1885-1915*, Jacaranda Press, Brisbane.

Murphy, D.J., Joyce, Roger B. & M.Cribb eds, 1990, *The premiers of Queensland*, rev. ed., UQPress, St Lucia.

Pope, David 1986, 'Protection & Australian manufacturers' international competitiveness: 1901-1930', *Australian economic history review*, 26: 21-39.

Powell, J.M. 1991, *Plains of promise, rivers of destiny: Water management and the development of Queensland, 1824-1990*, Boolarong Publications, Brisbane.

Powell J.M. & M. Williams eds, 1975, *Australian space, Australian time,* Oxford University Press, Melbourne.

Prentice, S.A. 1988, 'Edward Barton, pioneer electrical engineer', *Memoirs of the Queensland Museum* 27/1: 1-110.

Prentice, S.A. 1982, *Electricity in early Brisbane,* Institution of Engineers, Australia (Queensland Division), Queensland Division Technical Papers 23/19.

Queensland Employers Federation 1886-1914, Queensland Employers' Federation, Minutes of meetings, Film 0090 V1/C1, JOL.

Queensland Government, *Statistics of the State of Queensland,* 1900-30, Queensland Government Printer, Brisbane.

Queensland Government 1901, 'Report of the Registrar-General on Agricultural and Pastoral Statistics for 1900', QPP 4, 1901, Government Printer, Brisbane.

Rogan, R.G. 1992, *One hundred years of service,* BCC, Brisbane

Sachs, H.P.J. 1997a, *Abridged extracts from the Official Minute Books 1910–1997,* E. Sachs & Co. Pty. Ltd., Brisbane.

Sachs, H.P.J., 1997b, *Clara Sachs' Red Book Familie,* E. Sachs & Co. Pty. Ltd., Brisbane.

Sachs, H.P.J. 1997c, *The extracts: 100 years of history of E. Sachs & Co. Ltd. Vol. 2,* E. Sachs & Co. Pty. Ltd., Brisbane.

Sachs, H.P.J. 1997d, *The narrative: Recollections of part of the 100 years of history of E. Sachs & Co. Ltd. Vol. 1*, E. Sachs & Co. Pty. Ltd., Brisbane.

Simmers, J.M. 1992, *Electric lighting in Brisbane – the first decade 1882-1892: Lighting*, Institution of Engineers, Australia (Queensland Division), Queensland Division Technical Papers 33/5.

Steer, G.R. 1944, 'Brisbane tramways, their history and development', *Journal of the Historical Society of Queensland* 3/3:209-233.

Stubbs-Brown, Margaret 1962, The secondary industries of Queensland: 1875-1900, UQ BA hons thesis.

Watson, Don & Judith McKay 1994, *Queensland architects of the 19th century,* Queensland Museum, Brisbane.

Whitmore, Raymond L. ed. 1984, *Eminent Queensland engineers,* Institution of Engineers, Australia, Queensland Division.

Williams, M. 1975, 'More and smaller is better: Australian rural settlement 1788-1914', in Powell & Williams 1975.

Wiltshire, Kenneth 1980, 'Manufacturing', in Murphy, Joyce & Hughes, 1980.

Patriots and Protesters

Ackland, Michael, ed., 1993, *The Penguin book of 19th century Australian literature*, Penguin Books Australia, Melbourne.

Birchley, Delia 1978, The life and works of George Essex Evans (1863-1909), MA thesis, UQ.

Birrell, B. 2001, *Federation: The secret story*, Daffy & Snellgrove, Sydney.

Blake, H. Irwin 1900, 'How federation was won in Western Australia', *Review of reviews,* August 15: 167-70.

Brockett, Richard 1993, Douglas social credit in Queensland 1929-39, UQ PG Dip. of Arts thesis.

Browne, R. Spencer 1927, *A journalist's memories*, Read Press, Brisbane.

Deakin, Alfred, Papers, MS 1540, NLA, Canberra.

Evans, George Essex 1908, 'The poetry of Brunton Stephens', *Lone hand*, 1 Jan., 340-3.

Evans, George Essex 1928, *Collected verse of George Essex Evans*, Angus & Robertson, Sydney.

Evans, George Essex, Clippings and newspaper articles by and about George Essex Evans, Papers, PR 8207. v31 A6 1976, FL, UQ.

Evans, George Essex, Papers, UQ FL 13, FL, UQ.

Evans, George Essex, Papers, MS 79, NLA, Canberra.

Evans, Raymond 1985, 'Some furious outbursts of riots: Returned soldiers and Queensland's Red Flag disturbances', *War and society*, 3: 75-98.

Evans, Raymond 1986a, 'A bad time for balalaikas: Australia's first Red scare 1918-20', *The history teacher*, 39: 10-17.

Evans, Raymond 1986b, 'The battles of Brisbane: The conscription struggle 1916-1917', in BHG 1986.

Evans, Raymond 1987, *Loyalty and disloyalty. Social conflict on the Queensland homefront 1914-18*, Allen & Unwin, Sydney.

Evans, Raymond 1988, *The Red Flag riots. A study of intolerance*, UQ Press, St Lucia.

Evans, Raymond 1992, '"Agitation, ceaseless agitation": Russian radicals in Australia and the Red Flag riots', in Poole 1992, 126-71.

Evans, Raymond 1995, '"Social passion": Vere Gordon Childe in Queensland, 1918-19', in *Childe in Australia: Archaeology, politics and ideas*, ed. Peter Gathercole, T.H. Irving, Gregory Melleuish, 1-26.

Evans, Raymond 1999, *Fighting words. Writing about race*, UQ Press, St Lucia.

Evans, Raymond forthcoming, The politics of leprosy: Race, disease and the rise of Labor',

Evans, Raymond & J. Walker 1977, '"These strangers, where are they going?": Aboriginal-European relations in the Fraser Island and Wide Bay region 1770-1905', ed. P. Laver, *Fraser Island, Occasional papers in anthropology*, 8: 89-91.

Gathercole, Peter, Irving, T.H., & Gregory Melleuish 1995, *Childe in Australia, archaeology, politics and ideas*, UQ Press, St Lucia.

Green, H.M., 1966, *The history of Australian literature*, vol. 1, Angus & Robertson, Sydney.

Hadgraft, Cecil 1969, *James Brunton Stephens*, UQPress, St Lucia.

Harman, Kaye, ed. 1985, *Australia brought to book: Responses to Australia by visiting writers 1836-1939*, Boobook Publications, Balgowlah.

Hirst, J. 2000, *The sentimental nation: The making of the Australian Commonwealth*, Oxford University Press, Melbourne.

Irving, E.H. 1891, 'Two new Australian poets', *Australasian critic*, May: 174-76.

Irving, Helen, ed. 1999a, *The centenary companion to Australian federation*, Cambridge University Press, Melbourne.

Irving Helen, 1999b, *To constitute a nation: A cultural history of Australia's Constitution*, Cambridge University Press, Melbourne.

Kellow, H.A. 1930, *Queensland poets*, Harrap, London.

Kipling, Rudyard 1940, *Rudyard Kipling's verse: Definitive edition*, Hodder & Stoughton, London.

Kipling, Rudyard 1946, *Barrack room ballads and other verses*, Methuen, London.

La Nauze, John A. 1965, *Alfred Deakin: A biography*, Melbourne University Press, Melbourne.

Lindsay, Jack 1985, *The blood vote*, UQ Press, St Lucia.

Lindsay, Norma 1965, *Bohemians of the* Bulletin, Angus & Robertson, Sydney.

Magarey, Susan et al, eds. 1993, *Debutante nation: Feminism contests in the 1890s*, Allen & Unwin, St Leonards.

Malouf, David 1998 (1975), *Johnno*, UQ Press, St Lucia.

Meston, Archibald 1901a, Southern Aboriginal Protector's report, 1 Jul. QSA Col 143.

Meston, Archibald 1901b, Report, 23 Sep. QSA Col 144.

Palmer, Vance 1954, *The legend of the nineties*, Currey O'Neil Ross, Melbourne.

Poole Tom 1992, *Russia and the fifth continent: Aspects of Russian-Australian relations*, UQ Press, St Lucia.

Rolfe, Patricia 1979, *The journalistic javelin: An illustrated history of the* Bulletin, Wildcat Press, Sydney.

Stephens, Alfred George, comp. 1901, *The old* Bulletin *reader: The best stories from the* Bulletin *1881-1901*, The Bulletin Newspaper Company, Sydney.

Shaw, AlanG.L. 1990, 'Centennial reflections on Sir Henry Parkes' Tenterfield oration', *Canberra Historical Journal*, March: 3-10.

Stephens, James Brunton 1925, *The poetical works of James Brunton Stephens*, Angus & Robertson, Sydney.

Strahan, L. 1984, *Just city and the mirrors*: Meanjin *quarterly and the intellectual front*, Oxford University Press, Melbourne.

Stockwell, Stephen 2000, 'Wonderful progress: Alternative currents in colonial Brisbane', *Queensland review*, 7 (1 Aug.).

Tardent, Henry 1913, *The life and poetry of George Essex Evans*, H. Pole, Brisbane.

Thompson, P. & R. Macklin 2001. *The battle of Brisbane: Australians and Yanks at war*, ABC Books, Sydney.

Thorpe, William L. 1987, 'Class and politics in recent Queensland historiography: A Marxist critique', *Australian journal of politics and history* 33/1:19-29.

Tiffin, Chris 1991, 'Metaphor and emblem: George Essex Evans's public poetry', *The literary criterion*, 4/27:61-74.

Wallace, D.M. 1908, *The web of empire: A diary of the imperial tour of their royal highnesses, the Duke and Duchess of Cornwall and York in 1901*, Macmillan, London.

Wilde, William et al eds 1994, *The Oxford companion to Australian literature*, 2nd ed.

Wilson, Paul Douglas 1971, The Brisbane riot of September 1866', *Queensland heritage*, 2 (4 May):13-20.

Index

Note: Italics are used for pages with illustrations

Brisbane History Group Papers

Stylesheet for contributors

This serial, which focuses on the history and heritage of the Brisbane region, commenced in 1981. Each volume comprises papers given orally at BHG sessions and additional articles related in subject matter.

Contributors may be invited to submit papers for publication or inquire themselves whether a particular article would be acceptable in a forthcoming volume. Drafts should be forwarded to the publication coordinator for consideration by the editorial committee and referees. Inclusion does not preclude publication elsewhere for a different audience; but contributors are asked to discuss this with the coordinator and to acknowledge publication in the BHG Papers. Contributors receive one free copy of the whole volume.

The new series of papers from Number 11 onwards is typeset on personal computer, desktop designed, offset or docutech printed and produced as a custom-sized paperback in perfect binding. The print run of several hundred copies is marketed widely to members, libraries, schools, societies, professionals and the general public.

Contributors are asked to forward drafts shortly after the related BHG session. If a paper is given orally, it may be amended or reshaped as necessary. There is no strict word limit, as long as everything is pertinent to the subject and succinctly expressed. Notes and references are kept to an essential minimum. The onus is on the authors, not the editors, to provide a complete, accurate and presentable manuscript for publication.

Drafts should be submitted in single-spaced typing on A4 sized paper and if possible on 31/2 inch computer diskette in recent IBM compatible format (e.g. WordPerfect, Word or ASCII text file). They need to be set out in accordance with the BHG style of publication. Otherwise they may be returned to contributors for amendment.

The required publication style is exemplified by the BHG Papers from Number 11 onwards. The basic format for the end-notes and reference list is set out in the *Style Manual* of the Australian Government Publishing Service.

Notes are indicated in the text by running numbers placed after and above the nearest appropriate punctuation mark, and not by author and date in brackets. The notes themselves and the accompanying list of references are set out at the end using the author-date format, but omitting the abbreviations 'vol.', 'no.' and 'pp.' (e.g. 4/1:147-8 or 4:147-8).

The alphabetically arranged list of references includes all cited and useful works, except newspapers, lesser manuscripts and obvious printed sources already in the notes (with authors' family and given names (not initials), year plus small alpha-letter if more than one title by that author, titles of books with place and publisher, or titles of articles and serials with volume and page numbers).

Relevant illustrations of various kinds should be included with captions and sources stated, but these should be kept to an essential minimum. Good contrast, black and white copies are best, up to A4 in size (which may be reduced later). Letters of permission from the owners or repositories concerned are also needed for the BHG to reproduce (as a non-profit, community and educational association).

A cover sheet should be added with the contributor's preferred title, given and family names (not initials), and a sentence or two of self-description (e.g. occupation, status, positions, research activity, publications) for the contributors' page.

Please contact the publication coordinator regarding these matters, including particular requirements and queries. The BHG looks forward to publishing papers by amateur, public and academic historians as professionally and beneficially as possible.

Dr Barry Shaw
Publication Coordinator
(07) 3353 2309 (after hours)

Brisbane History Group
PO Box 12
Kelvin Grove DC, Q4059

Brisbane History Group Publications

Papers

1 *Brisbane: Public, practical, personal*, 1981
2 *Brisbane: Archives and approaches*, 1983
3 *Brisbane: Housing, health, the river and the arts*, 1985
4 *Brisbane at war*, 1986
5 *Brisbane: Aboriginal, alien, ethnic*, 1987
6 *Brisbane: People, places and pageantry*, 1987
7 *Brisbane: Archives and approaches II*, 1988
8 *Brisbane in 1888: The historical perspective*, 1988
9 *Brisbane: Local, oral and placename history*, 1990
10 *Brisbane: Mining, building, Story Bridge, the Windmill*, 1991
11 *Brisbane: The Aboriginal presence 1824-1860*, 1992
12 *Brisbane: The ethnic presence since the 1850s*, 1993
13 *Brisbane: Cemeteries as sources*, 1994
14 *Brisbane: People, places and progress*, 1995
15 *Brisbane: Corridors of power*, 1996
16 *Brisbane: Squatters, surveyors and settlers*, 2000
17 *Brisbane: Relaxation, recreation and rock'n'roll – popular culture 1890-1990*, 2001
18 *Brisbane: Patriotism, passion and protest – Our Federation 1901*, 2001

Sources

1 *Brisbane by 1888: The public image*, 1987
2 *The Brisbane Courier in 1888: A select subject index*, 1987
3 *Brisbane Town news from the Sydney Morning Herald 1842-46*, 1989
4 *Brisbane butterflies and beetles*, 1989
5 *Brisbane River Valley 1841-50*, 1991
6 *Brisbane hotels and publicans index 1842-1900*, 1994
7 *Qld architects of the 19th century: Index to the biographical dictionary*, 1999
8 *Brisbane timeline: From Captain Cook to Citycat*, 1999
9 *Moreton Bay in the news 1841-60: A select subject index*, 2000

Tours

1 *Petrie-Terrace walk/drive, 1981* rev. 1989
2 *South Brisbane civic precinct walk*, 1985, 1986
3 *South Brisbane: Southbank suburbs drive*, 1986
4 *Caboolture to Kilcoy drive*, 1986
5 *Town to Toowong riverpath walk*, 1986
6 *Brisbane 1888 drive*, 1988
7 *Eastern suburbs placenames drive*, 1990
8 *Sandgate and Shorncliffe walks*, 1990
9 *Old Coorparoo Shire drive*, 1991
10 *Brisbane River Valley drive*, 1991
11 *Colonial George and William Street walk*, 1991
12 *Spring Hill walk: St Pauls to Gregory Terrace*, 1993
13 *Bald Hills drive*, 1993
14 *Kedron drive*, 1993
15 *Brisbane city churches walk/drive*, 1994
16 *Stafford and Wilston-Grange drive*, 1995
17 *Brisbane historical pub drive*, 1995
18 *Yeronga heritage walk/drive*, 1996
19 *Spring walk: Wickham Terrace*, 1997
20 *St Lucia Campus walk*, 1998
21 *Stombuco heritage tour*, 1999
22 *Our federation 1901: Brisbane heritage trail*, 2001

Studies

1 *Brisbane's forgotten founder: Sir Evan Mackenzie of Kilcoy*, 1992
2 *Brisbane house styles 1880-1940: A guide to the affordable house*, 1998.

Information about the BHG and its publications may be obtained by letter or phone or by visiting the BHG web page http://www.brisbanehistory.asn.au